St. Louis Community College

Forest Park
Florissant Valley
Meramec

Instructional Resources
St. Louis, Missouri

GAYLORD

The Fantastic Sublime

**Recent Titles in Contributions to the
Study of Science Fiction and Fantasy**

The Fantastic Sublime

Romanticism and Transcendence in Nineteenth-Century Children's Fantasy Literature

DAVID SANDNER

Contributions to the Study of Science Fiction and Fantasy,
Number 69
C. W. Sullivan III, Series Adviser

GREENWOOD PRESS
Westport, Connecticut • London

Library of Congress Cataloging-in-Publication Data

Sandner, David.
    The fantastic sublime : romanticism and transcendence in
nineteenth-century children's fantasy literature / David Sandner.
        p. cm. — (Contributions to the study of science fiction and
fantasy, ISSN 0193–6875 ; no. 69)
    Includes bibliographical references and index.
    ISBN 0–313–30084–4 (alk. paper)
    1. Children's literature, English—History and criticism.
2. English literature—19th century—History and criticism.
3. Fantastic literature, English—History and criticism.
4. Children—Books and reading—History—19th century.
5. Transcendence (Philosophy) in literature. 6. Sublime, The, in
literature. 7. Romanticism—Great Britain. I. Title. II. Series.
PR990.S26 1996
823′.08766099282—dc20   96–5805

British Library Cataloguing in Publication Data is available.

Library of Congress Catalog Card Number: 96–5805
ISBN: 0–313–30084–4
ISSN: 0193–6875

First published in 1996

Greenwood Press, 88 Post Road West, Westport, CT 06881
An imprint of Greenwood Publishing Group, Inc.

Printed in the United States of America

The paper used in this book complies with the
Permanent Paper Standard issued by the National
Information Standards Organization (Z39.48–1984).

10 9 8 7 6 5 4 3 2 1

Contents

Acknowledgments

I want to thank my committee, Professors Wai-Leung Kwok, George Tuma and Gary Mathews of San Francisco State University, for their comments and advice during the early drafts of this work. I wish to express gratitude to Professor C.W. Sullivan III of East Carolina University for steering me towards sources I would otherwise have missed. I also want to thank my colleagues at the University of Oregon: Barbara Hewick, Michael Arnzen and Chris Hitt for copy editing and Chris Hitt and Kathleen McHugh for technical support beyond the call of duty.

I also want to thank my parents, Mary and Donald, for providing, as Mole would say, "some anchorage in one's existence." I especially want to thank Jill Roberts for emergency copy editing and, most of all, for putting up with me. I love you.

PART I

ROMANTICISM, CHILDHOOD, FAIRY TALES AND THE WORLD OF THE SPIRIT

Chapter 1

Puer Aeternus, the Divine Child

Lewis Carroll invented *Alice in Wonderland* (1865) for Alice Liddell while boating one "golden afternoon," writing it down only after Alice insisted (Gardner, 21-4). Kenneth Grahame began *The Wind in the Willows* (1908) as a bedtime story for his son Alastair. He continued the story in a series of letters, only later turning the letters, fortunately saved by Alastair's governess, into a book (Gooderson, 8-11). John Ruskin wrote *The King of the Golden River* (1851), one of the first English literary fairy tales, simply "to amuse a little girl," twelve-year-old Effie Gray (Coyle, 86).

So many Victorian and Edwardian fantasies began as larks, extempore romances for the delight of children, written down by chance, that one dominant trope of nineteenth-century children's fantasy literature is its seeming unimportance. Moral tales, the primary children's literature of the eighteenth and early nineteenth centuries, were books of instruction, written with a manifest purpose: to help children become adults. In counterpoint, nineteenth-century children's fantasy presented itself as oral, told in a moment of childlike spontaneity, as without purpose except delight, as reveling in the imagination—what cannot be seen and what cannot be taught.

Nineteenth-century children's fantasy was written not simply *to* but *for* children, either for a specific child or a general, ephemeral childlike quality in adults. In his letters Oscar Wilde wrote that his fairy tales were "meant partly for children, and partly for those who have kept the child-like faculties of wonder and joy" (219). George MacDonald wrote not "for children, but for the childlike, whether five, or fifty, or seventy-five" ("Fantastic Imagination," 317). Wilde's and MacDonald's statements, unremarkable now, marked at the time a deliberate contrast to what had come a century before. In the nineteenth-century, childhood became not just what one left behind but also what one lost by growing up.

Considering works by William Wordsworth and Samuel Taylor Coleridge, I will examine the ways in which Romantic poetry took part in a revolution of the eighteenth-century view of childhood and of fantasy. Romanticism brought about changes in society's image of children, the purpose of reading, and the importance of the imagination, opening the way for children's fantasy to become a popular and commercially successful genre. Nineteenth-century children's fantasy, in turn, displayed many hallmarks of its Romantic heritage—the visionary, pantheism, the wise child, the imagination unbound. From Alice in *Alice in Wonderland* (1865) to Max in Maurice Sendak's *Where the Wild Things Are* (1963), the visionary child, the child of the Romantic sublime, has held a central place in children's literature.

Looking at a collection of Victorian and Edwardian children's fantasies, George MacDonald's *At the Back of the North Wind* (1871), Kenneth Grahame's *The Wind in the Willows* (1908) and Christina Rossetti's *Goblin Market* (1862), I will examine the ways in which nineteenth-century fantasy for children participated in a significant extension and revision of the Romantic sublime. Nineteenth-century children's fantasy, in what I will call the "fantastic sublime," both continued and remade the tradition of the revelatory moment when the imagination, often in communion with nature, reveals a transcendent purpose.

At first glance, the relationship between Romantic poetry and nineteenth-century children's fantasy literature may seem abstruse. As literary movements, Romanticism and children's fantasy did not significantly overlap. In the early part of the nineteenth century, the Romantics "rediscovered" fantasy and wrote new works that boldly explored its possibilities, especially the once-popular but often badly written "Gothic" fantasy of the previous century. All of the major English Romantic poets, Blake, Wordsworth, Byron, Shelley and

Keats, wrote works of fantastic literature. Coleridge especially wrote works of what he called "Faery." The "Rime of the Ancient Mariner," "Kubla Khan" and "Christabel" are prime examples of his work as a Gothic fantasist. But the Romantics wrote for adults and their fantasies had adult concerns. Many of Coleridge's "Faery" poems were released jointly with Wordsworth's naturalistic poems in the one project of *The Lyrical Ballads* (1798), a work aimed at and written for a literate, adult audience. In his book *The Romantic Fantastic*, the critic Tobin Siebers examines prominent Romantic prose authors from many countries who wrote adult fantastic literature that Siebers calls "superstitious" but which could as easily be called "Gothic": he names E.T.A. Hoffmann and Goethe in Germany; Sir Walter Scott in England; Gérald de Nerval and Prosper Mérimée in France; Nikoli Gogol and Alexander Pushkin in Russia; Nathanial Hawthorne and Edgar Allan Poe in America (23-4). His list is only partial, but demonstrates the force and skill of the serious adult Romantic writers turning to the fantastic as a form in the late eighteenth and early nineteenth century. But the Gothic, reserved largely for adolescents today, belonged to adults in the eighteenth and nineteenth centuries (Manlove, *Impulse*, 4).

Most works, and the most enduring, of nineteenth-century children's fantasy appeared following the mid-century, after the intensity of Romanticism had waned in adult works. And children's fantasy's direct literary antecedents lie not in English Romantic poetry, but in fairy tales, especially the collected folk and fairy tales and literary fairy tales of Germany. The critic C.N. Manlove claims:

Nineteenth-century fantasy sprang from two main sources: revived interest in the traditional fairy or folk tale and the German Romantic fairy tales of Novalis, Hoffman, Tieck and de la Motte Fouque, the latter written mostly around the period 1795-1820. ("Victorian and Modern Fantasy," 9)

Pointing to these sources alone, however, does not explain the rise of fantastic literature for children. In England, interest in traditional fairy tales revived after the appearance of *Kinder- und Hausmärchen* (1812-1815) by the Brothers Grimm, translated from 1823-1826. However, the English folklorists, who followed the lead of the Brothers Grimm in a publishing boom of scholarly fairy tale collections in the 1820s, intended their works for adults (Manlove, *Impulse*, 2). The German Romantics, considered among the first to invent original literary fairy tales and to use fairy tale materials in their stories (Egoff, 33), also wrote, as with their Gothic work (the Gothic and the fairy being, for them, often one and the same thing), for an adult audience. Before fairy tales could give rise to children's fantasy, childhood itself, and what was considered appropriate for children, had to change. Manlove comments:

Although the German Romantics and the scholar helped to give new status to the fairy tale, it was children and what was thought suitable reading matter for them that in England at least caused the explosion of its popularity. (*Impulse*, 2)

The English Romantic poets, especially Wordsworth, helped redefine the image of childhood in relation to what the critic Ross Woodman calls "the *puer aeternus*, the divine child" (72). Marie-Louise von Franz explains the origins and implications of the term:

Puer aeternus is the name of a god of antiquity. The words themselves come from Ovid's *Metamorphoses* and are there applied to the child-god in the Elusinian mysteries. Ovid speaks of the child-god Iacchus, addressing him as *puer aeternus* and praising him in his role in these mysteries. In later times, the child-god was identified with Dionysus and the god Eros. He is the divine youth who is born in the night in this typical mother-cult mystery of Eleusis, and who is a redeemer. (Franz, 1)

The Romantic child is also a redeemer. For the Romantics, the sacred innocence and imagination of childhood offered redemption to fallen adulthood. Wordsworth wrote: "trailing clouds of glory do we come/ From God, who is our home:/ Heaven lies about us in our infancy!/ Shades of the prison-house begin to close/ Upon the growing Boy" ("Ode: Intimations," 64-8). Wordsworth's vision of the wise child, the child of glory, marked a sharp contrast to the earlier prevalent view that children were sinful and needed correction (Darton, 85; Watson, "Coleridge," 14). Woodman argues in his paper, "The Idiot Boy as Healer," that Wordsworth, following a deep depression over the collapse of the French Revolution, turned inward to "the real revolution, overthrowing the corrupted taste of an *ancien regime* and replacing it with a true republic of the soul presided over by a divine child" (72-5). Woodman claims this "inner revolution [of the divine child]. . .changed the course of English literature even as the French revolution changed the course of history" (72).

The critic Humphrey Carpenter, in his book *Secret Gardens: A Study of the Golden Age of Children's Literature*, also claims that Wordsworth's poetry changed the image of childhood and so altered the course of English literature, and children's literature in particular. Carpenter calls Wordsworth's "Ode: Intimations of Immortality," published in 1807:

> a call to revolution against the view of childhood which had persisted throughout the eighteenth century, a view which had dominated both education and the writing of children's books. (7)

As Carpenter points out, three of the most important eighteenth-century writers on childhood, the philosopher John Locke, the writer Rousseau and the educator Mrs. Sarah Trimmer, all, despite many other differences, wrote about the dangers of "giving children reading matter that would merely excite the imagination" (7). The Romantic poets, although some of their works, like Blake's *Songs of Innocence* or Coleridge's "Rime of the Ancient Mariner," have been published in later times in editions meant for children, did not write for children; but they changed the course of its history nevertheless simply by embracing the imagination and linking it positively with childhood. Carpenter describes the shift in values that Romantic poetry effected in children's literature as sudden and decisive:

> The greater number of children's books published in England between the 1740s and the 1820s were sternly moral, using simple stories to convey whatever ethical message was then in fashion, whether it be that hard work always leads to improvement . . . or that idle and thoughtless children would soon die . . . and . . . suffer everlasting torment in Hell. . . .
> The Romantics view of childhood turned this upside down. (7)

Carpenter finds in the early Romantic poet William Blake's *Songs of Innocence*, published in 1789, the "first stirrings of change" in a poetry that was "an ardent affirmation that children have access to a kind of visionary simplicity that is denied to adults" (8). After the Romantic poets, adults turn to children as a means to experience the innocent world of the spirit. Blake's front-piece poem calls his "happy songs" those that "Every child may joy to hear" (lines 19-20). Carpenter comments: "Adults, it is implied, will not have the same instinctive understanding of their visions. Nine years later came the *Lyrical Ballads*, to which Wordsworth contributed several poems describing the child's view of the world" (8). Carpenter points, by way of example, to Wordsworth's "Anecdote for Fathers," which "celebrates a child's simple directness of thought," particularly in its concluding stanza:

> O dearest, dearest boy! my heart
> For better lore would seldom yearn
> Could I but teach the hundredth part
> Of what from thee I learn. (57-60)

In Romantic works, the adult moves from teacher to student, from stern moralizing to the undisciplined child to patient listening to the wise instruction of the simple and imaginative child. For Carpenter, the promise of the Romantic child in Blake's *Songs of Innocence* and Wordsworth's *Lyrical Ballads* is finally fulfilled in Wordsworth's, to give the full title, "Ode: Intimations of Immortality from Recollections of Early Childhood," a poem in which the image of childhood becomes a divine image (8). The Romantics, especially Wordsworth, and especially, if Woodman and Carpenter are to be believed, Wordsworth's "Ode: Intimations of Immortality," rewrote the adult understanding of childhood and the imagination, precipitating, in a short time, a complete revolution in the acceptance of fantastic literature for children.

Romanticism's new view of the imagination as a positive creative force—"My shaping spirit of Imagination" ("Dejection," line 86) as Coleridge called it—its new view of poetry as "proposing for its *immediate* object pleasure, not truth" (Coleridge, *Biographia*, 2:13) and, especially, its new view of childhood as sacred, all promoted the legitimacy of fantasy for children. By the middle of the nineteenth century, the Romantic view, watered down and sentimentalized, had sifted into the popular imagination (Egoff, 37-8), and children's literature would never be the same.

The shift toward the fantastic in children's literature occurred rapidly over the first half of the nineteenth century. The scholarly fairy tale collections of the 1820s begot new collections increasingly aimed at children as the century wore on (Manlove, *Impulse*, 2-3; Egoff, 33). Hans Christian Andersen's popular fairy tales, *Wonderful Stories for Children* (1846), perhaps even more than the literary fairy tales of the German Romantics, prompted imitative English literary fairy tales for children (Egoff, 41). Evidence suggests John Ruskin delayed publishing *The King of the Golden River* (1851), one of the first English literary fairy tales for children, for ten years until the popularity of Andersen's stories convinced him his story would find an audience (Prickett, 66).

A vogue of pretty nonsense verse around the turn of the nineteenth century, set off by "The Butterfly's Ball and the Grasshopper's Feast" (1807) by William Roscoe (Darton, 199-202), and the popularity of the "Christmas pantomime" for children in the 1840s-50s, following the success of Dickens' *Christmas Carol* (1843) and Thackery's *The Rose and the Ring* (1855), also promoted wide acceptance of children's fantasy by mid-century (Prickett, 45-6; Egoff, 41). For the first time, children's authors wrote to please children without trying to improve them. Edward Lear's *Book of Nonsense* (1846) and Carroll's *Alice* (1865) celebrated childhood, for the Romantic child had a purity and incandescent power that had only faded in the adult.

The revolutionary Romantic view of childhood promoted, and was promoted by, the image of childhood in children's literature, whether realistic or fantastic literature. As one critic remarks of nineteenth-century American children's literature (and the same holds for English children's literature):

When the journey was complete, the children of children's fiction, rational, sober, and imperfect at the beginning of the nineteenth-century had become innocent, charming, and perfect: the rational child had become the romantic child. (MacLeod, 141)

By the middle of the nineteenth century, the visionary romantic child is everywhere, including adult literature. The critic Humphrey Carpenter writes that both Jane Austen's *Jane Eyre* (1847) and Charlotte Brontë's *Wuthering Heights* (1847) "accept that children have a clear, even heightened, vision of the world" (9). Carpenter lists George Eliot's *The Mill on the Floss* (1860) and *Silas Marner* (1861) as other prominent examples of nineteenth-century adult works that present

Romantic notions of childhood, and points especially, "more than any other novelist of this period," to Charles Dickens (9-10). Carpenter describes Dickens' *Oliver Twist* as the prototype for a flood of nineteenth-century "novels in which orphan waifs were leading their elders spiritually by the hand and inculcating in them a true love of God" (10). The divine child became an important figure for a locus of adult feeling and anxiety over the numinous.

In children's fantasy literature, the Romantic child is Lewis Carroll's sweet, unflappable Alice, "Child of the pure unclouded brow/ And dreaming eyes of wonder!" (Carroll, 173, lines 1-2). Her polite astonishment and curiosity in a topsy-turvy world of nonsense aptly express the relation of bewildered childhood to the sometimes implacably repressive, sometimes madly violent world of adulthood. The Romantic child is Francis Browne's Childe Charity in *Granny's Wonderful Chair* (1856), whose loving kindness in a thoughtless world—giving up her supper and bed to an ungrateful old beggar for seven nights and taking care of the beggar's ugly dog—redeems adult humanity in the eyes of Fairyland. In the end, the dog and beggar reveal themselves to be:

"a prince and princess of Fairyland, and there was a wager between us whether or not there were good people still to be found in these false and greedy times. One said 'Yes,' and the other said 'No'; and I have lost," said the prince, "and must pay the feasts and presents." (86)

The Romantic child is George MacDonald's Diamond in *At the Back of the North Wind* (1871), who is called "God's Baby" because of his simplicity and wisdom and whose acts of self-sacrifice and visionary power take him back of the north wind. His premature death from "wasting away" seems the only possible end for such a precious, perfect child utterly unfit for "fallen" adulthood. The Romantic child reaches perhaps its apotheosis in Oscar Wilde's literary fairy tale "The Selfish Giant" (1888). The Selfish Giant closes his magical garden off and chases away children who get in to climb in his trees until one day through a window he spies a little boy:

so small he could not reach up to the branches of the tree, and he was wandering all around it, crying bitterly. . . .

And the Giant's heart melted as he looked out. "How selfish I have been!" he said; "now I know why Spring would not come here. I will put that poor little boy on the top of the tree, and then I will knock down the wall, and my garden shall be the children's playground for ever and ever." (298)

Having redeemed the Giant (adult), the boy leaves and does not return until years later, still as a little boy, but this time as the Christ child himself, "on the palms of his hands . . . the prints of two nails, and the prints of two nails . . . on his little feet" (299), come to take the Giant to Paradise. In the moral tale, the adults had instructed the children in ethics and right behavior; in nineteenth-century children's fantasy, now the corrupted adults must follow the children to heaven—only childhood, through the purity of innocence and the force of imagination, could redeem fallen humanity.

Chapter 2

"Old" Fairy Tales and the "New" Romantic Child

Wilde's sentimental treatment of childhood in "The Selfish Giant" is typical not only of literary fairy tales, but of actual fairy tales as edited and rewritten throughout the nineteenth century. Until the boom of fairy tale collections in England in the early nineteenth century, led by the success of the Brothers Grimm, few fairy tales had been written down. However, early extant collections, as well as manuscript versions and first editions of the tales as collected in the nineteenth century, suggest that the oral tales were bawdier, more whimsical and raucous than the versions of the tales with which we are familiar; they were told to young and old and, judging from the sources used by the Brothers Grimm (Zipes, "Introduction," xxiv), belonged to all classes.

"Like a fairy tale" has come to mean a beautiful, wish-fulfilling dream or fantasy, especially the fulfillment of romantic love, and a happy ending, but actual fairy tales as recorded by the Brothers Grimm in the early nineteenth century meditate at least as much, or more, on unhappiness—on helplessness, victimization, violence, revenge, murder, mutilation, cannibalism, infanticide and incest—as on happy endings (Tatar, *Hard*, xxi, 4; Opie, 11). Subsequent editions of the tales were edited to be more suitable for children alone, childhood itself becoming more clearly defined—and more starkly divided from adulthood—in the process. Thus, when Victorian writers wrote the first English literary fairy tales, they wrote magical adventures with happy endings, completing the transformation of the fairy tale, no matter what it had been once upon a time, into what it is commonly understood to be now.

However, the Grimms' project began as a scholarly patriotic venture, meant not for children but for academic colleagues: "Weighed down by a ponderous introduction and by extensive annotations, the first edition of the *Nursery and Household Tales* had the look of a scholarly tome, rather than of a book for a wide audience" (Tatar, *Hard*, 11). The first English translation of the *Household Tales* by Edgar Taylor in 1823 presented a selection of tales chosen and edited exclusively for children. For the first time, fairy tales were meant for children alone (Tatar, *Hard*, xiv). The success of that volume expedited the Grimms' own rapid transformation of the fairy tales (Tatar, 19).

In subsequent editions, the Grimms fleshed out the texts with description, sometimes doubling their original length, polished the "crude country" prose, eliminated the preface and notes, added illustrations and deleted unsuitable material (Tatar, 16-20). The stories were essentially recast, both extended and emended, for children. But fairy tales had been told to children all along. The oral tales had belonged to everyone. The fairy tales were not the only thing changing; the image of childhood itself was being recast by the new dominant middle-class buying public. According to Jack Zipes, the Brothers Grimm

eliminated erotic and sexual elements that might be offensive to middle-class morality, added numerous Christian expressions and references, [and] emphasized specific role models for male and female protagonists according to the dominant patriarchal code of that time. ("Introduction," xxviii)

For example, in the original manuscript version of "Snow White," the dwarves ask only that she "do the cooking for them when they went to mines" ("Introduction," xxvi). Beginning with the first 1812 edition of the *Household Tales*, the dwarves "pose different terms for the contract, terms that no doubt reflect the Grimms' notions on contractual relations between men and women" (Tatar, *Hard*, 29): "If you'll keep the house for us, cook, make the beds, wash, sew and knit, and if you'll keep everything neat and orderly, you can stay with us, and we'll provide you with everything you need" (Grimm, 199). The traditional roles of men and women became more sharply defined as the fairy tales became the exclusive domain of children. In other words, the new Romantic view of childhood, despite its celebration of the imagination unbound, had another side, more rigid and disturbing. The cherishing of childhood innocence meant the forsaking of adult understanding. The nineteenth-century literary world of childhood was not only simplified, but codified, even stifled, according to the dominant cultural beliefs of what was and what was not appropriate for children.

The roles of the sexes in the fairy tales came under strict review. Often, this meant the women in the tales becoming ever more passive and the men more active. As one critic discovered after close study of the Grimms' editing of dialogue in "Cinderella":

this tale shows that he [Wilhelm Grimm] did not simply animate early versions of the tales by replacing indirect with direct speech. Instead, a detailed analysis reveals that Grimm removed direct speech from women and gave it to men. (Bottigheimer, 59)

Further, the direct speech left to female characters "tended to be transferred . . . from good to bad girls and women" (58). The Grimms actually magnified "female villainy in successive editions of the stories they had collected" (Tatar, *Off*, 232). As the critic Ruth B. Bottigheimer writes:

A general pattern of exculpating men and incriminating women permeates *Grimms' Tales*. This pattern is clearly evident in the post 1819 versions of "Hansel and Gretel," "Snow White" and "Cinderella," each of which provides a stepmother who assumes the burden of blame while the father, virtually absent, shoulders no share of the responsibility for his children's fates. (81)

The prevalence of wicked stepmothers in fairy tales (not simply the presence of the wicked stepmothers, that you *can* find anywhere) is wholly attributable to the Brothers Grimm. As the preponderance of mothers in the tales became villains, the Grimms shifted some of the mothers to step-mothers. From the first to second edition versions, the Grimms replaced the biological mother of "Snow White" with a stepmother (Tatar, *Hard*, 24; 36; 143). In the fourth edition, the mother of "Hansel and Gretel" makes the same change (Tatar, 36).

The cruel mother or stepmother may seem to be the natural dominant childhood fear, given the prominence of women in child rearing, but if early variations of fairy tales can be credited, fathers inspired at least a comparable fear. Maria Tatar comments:

What seems more likely is that the men who recorded these oral tales—and for the most part the great collectors of the nineteenth-century were male—showed, whenever they had a choice, a distinct preference for stories with female villains over tales with male giants and ogres. (Tatar, *Off*, 233)

As a corollary, collectors also showed a preference for tales with passive heroines. The critic Alison Lurie points out that editors of the great nineteenth-century fairy tale collections preferred "Snow White," "Cinderella," "Sleeping Beauty" and "Little Red Ridinghood" over other available tales with "strong, brave, clever, and resourceful heroines" (xi-xiii). The oral tales had existed in many variations with incidental details, including gender, often reversed. Nineteenth-century editors restricted the variations simply by choosing what to write down and what to pass by, biasing the stories even before editing the texts of the tales.

In response to middle-class mores, women in fairy tales became not only more passive, but more chaste. In a copy of the original 1810 draft of "The Frog King, or Iron Heinrich," when the princess dashes the helpless frog against the wall, "he hit the wall, . . . fell down into the bed and lay there, a handsome young prince, then the princess lay down with him" (Bottigheimer, 160). In the first 1812 edition of the *Household Tales*, the prince still falls in the bed, but we are told he became "her dear companion" (Bottigheimer, 161) and they immediately fell "peacefully asleep" (Tatar, *Hard*, 8). After the second edition, the reader is not told where the prince landed, only that the transformation took place when he hit the wall. Wedding vows are exchanged, with the express approval of her father the king, before the couple retires to bed (Grimm, 4). Maria Tatar comments:

The Grimms' transformation of a tale replete with sexual innuendo into a prim and proper nursery story with a dutiful daughter is almost as striking as the folkloric metamorphosis of frog into prince. (*Hard*, 8)

The complete removal of any hint of sex is probably the single most universal emendation of the tales by editors during the nineteenth century. In eighteenth-century French versions of "Little Red Riding Hood," the heroine performs a slow striptease for the wolf (Darnton, 9-10). Her clothes are put into a fire, because she will not need them anymore, first her apron, then her bodice, dress skirt and hose. This striptease does not appear at all in, for example, Andrew Lang's celebrated 1889 collection, *The Blue Fairy Book* (51-3).

Incest, involving both sex and a villainous father, especially distressed the Grimms and "incest" tales had to be either eliminated altogether, the offending scenes edited out, or judgmental commentary added in (Tatar, *Hard*, 8-9). In early versions of the appalling "The Maiden Without Hands," incest motivates the heroine to leave home (Tatar, 10-1). In later editions of the *Household Tales*, the incest has been removed. Thus the Maiden, her motivation confounded, sets out into the world without reason or purpose.

Pregnancy, as incontrovertible evidence of sex, also came under editorial review. The story of "Hans Dumm," who impregnates a princess just by thinking about it, is included in the first edition of the *Household Tales* but cut from the second (Tatar, *Hard*, 7). Also in the first edition, Rapunzel is impregnated by the prince who dallies in her tower. Her secret trysts are discovered when she asks: "Tell me, Godmother, why my clothes are so tight and why they don't fit any longer." In the second edition, the pregnancy is removed: "Tell me, Godmother, why is it that you are much harder to pull up than the young prince?" (Tatar, *Hard*, 18; Zipes, "Introduction," xxvi-xxvii).

In the original "The Master Hunter," a variant of "Sleeping Beauty" found only in the Grimms' notes, the story's hero enters a tower, discovers a naked princess asleep on her bed, and lies down with her. Later, the princess is discovered to be pregnant, to her father's distress (Tatar, *Hard*, 7). The version the Grimms printed is restrained and decorous, completely without the unwanted pregnancy or sexual contact of any kind (Grimm, 404).

In Giambattista Basile's racy seventeenth-century Neapolitan version of "Sleeping Beauty," a king comes upon sleeping beauty and rapes her. She becomes pregnant and awakens not by a kiss, but by the suckling of the twin children to which she has given birth (Opie, 81). Because, as in Charles Perrault's version of the tale, the illicit children figure prominently in the plot of "Sleeping Beauty," as, for example, when the wicked ogre-mother of the prince attempts to eat them, the pregnancy remained in the tale into the nineteenth century, but only under the condition of marriage. In Andrew Lang's *The Blue Fairy Book* (1889), Sleeping Beauty magically awakens at the prince's approach and "after supper, without losing any time, the lord almoner married them in the chapel of the castle, and the chief lady of the honour drew the curtains" (Lang, 59-60). With those vows, however, a two-century transformation of the prince's affections is complete. In Basile's seventeenth-century version, the prince is already married and it is his jealous wife, not his ogre-mother, who orders her rival's children cooked and eaten (Opie, 81-3). Edition by edition, the first wife vanished, replaced by an ogre who is made to be the prince's mother, then the rape of Sleeping Beauty vanished, replaced by marriage, as the illicit extramarital sex was legitimized even at the cost of sense and motivation in the story. After all, the wife's jealousy, while inexcusable, is a comprehensible motivation, and hence more frightening in its impact than the unfocused rapacity of the invented monster, the ogre-mother.

Violence, unlike sex, was not always removed. In fact, the Brothers Grimm only occasionally toned down violence, rather, they usually intensified it (Tatar, *Hard*, 5), especially when those who suffered it deserved it because of their moral outlook (Ellis, 79). As the critic Maria Tatar points out, where the Grimms "systematically purged the collection of references to sexuality and masked depictions of incestuous desire. . . . lurid portrayals of child abuse, starvation and exposure, like fastidious descriptions of cruel punishments, on the whole escaped censorship" (Tatar, *Hard*, 10-11).

In Perrault's earlier but more literary "Cinderella," the stepsisters only "did all they possibly could to thrust their foot into the Slipper, but they could not effect it" (127). In the Grimms' story, when the sisters cannot get their feet in the shoe, their mother hands them a knife and the first sister cuts her toe off and the second cuts off her heel. Each tries to ride away with the prince, but a bird sings:

Looky, look, look
at the shoe that she took.
There's blood all over, and her foot's too small.
She's not the bride you met at the ball. (Grimm, 91)

The prince, when he sees "blood oozing," returns the sisters and retrieves Cinderella. An incidental failure has become a grisly mutilation and revenge for the wickedness of the sisters.

At the end of Perrault's tale, the new Queen Cinderella forgave her sisters "with all her heart, and desired them always to love her" (Perrault, 127). Cinderella even "married them . . . to two great lords." Even in the first 1812 edition of the *Household Tales*, Cinderella's stepsisters are only "horrified" and "turn pale" at Cinderella's good turn in fortune (Tatar, *Off*, 7). By the second 1819 edition (Tatar, 5-6), pigeons peck out their eyes when "the two false sisters came to ingratiate themselves and share in Cinderella's good fortune" with the added justification: "Thus they were punished with blindness for the rest of their lives due to their wickedness and malice" (Grimm, 92).

A righteousness and wrath inform these changes, a belief that the right must not only prevail, but wickedness must be punished. As the increased rigidity of sexual roles—active heroes and passive heroines, evil old women at the root of all troubles—revealed one shadow side to the Romantic child of light, the increased violence of the tales reveals another. The Brothers Grimm, in their zeal for childhood innocence, imagined a world of justice with a vengeance.

Only to a lesser extent, and only after the Grimms, did nineteenth-century fairy tale editors work to show that the corollary held true: that steadfastness and bravery must be rewarded. In Taylor's translation of the Grimms' "Twelve Dancing Princesses," the suitor who fails to discover where the princesses go at night had his head cut off, and that was that! Iona and Peter Opie comment on these decapitations:

The do-or-die terms offered to candidates for a princess's hand are not uncommon in popular literature, but Victorian editors found their harshness unacceptable. In the age of self-help, it was not thinkable that those who strove and failed should be worse off than those who had never striven. (188)

The Opies point to Andrew Lang's version of "The Twelve

Dancing Princesses" as typical of nineteenth-century emendations of the tale. In his *The Red Fairy Book* (1890), Andrew Lang changed the grisly deaths of the suitors into the decorous (although to those in-the-know, still somewhat sinister) ending: "when the morning came they had all disappeared, and no one could tell what had become of them" (3).

Madame d'Aulnoy's eighteenth-century "Yellow Dwarf" ends unhappily with the death of the two innocent lovers at the hands of the cruel dwarf. When Walter Crane illustrated the story in 1875, the dwarf darted forward to kill the King of the Gold Mines, but his love, the princess, shrieked and the king turned.

With one blow he slew the wicked Dwarf, and then conducted the Princess to the sea-shore, where the friendly Syren was waiting to convey them to the Queen.   On their arrival at the palace, the wedding took place, and Toutebelle cured of her vanity, lived happily with the King of the Gold Mines. (Opie, 67)

In a collection called *Grimm's Goblins* (1861) the princess attacks the Yellow Dwarf's beard with magic scissors after which the King of the Gold Mines cuts off the Yellow Dwarf's head (Opie, 69).

In Perrault's version of "Little Red Riding Hood," the young heroine is eaten at the end. Later collectors of the tale, however, have disagreed with that ending. Indeed, whether Red Ridinghood lives, and if she does, whether her grandmother will be allowed to live as well, and who will save them, has been a matter of lively debate in the many different nineteenth-century versions of the tale (Opie, 94). The older version of "Little Red Riding Hood" does, however, contain certain gruesome details that nineteenth-century collectors reliably eliminated, even if they kept Red's abrupt and unfortunate demise. In an Italian version, the wolf kills the mother, makes a latch cord of her tendons, a meat pie of her flesh and wine from her blood. The heroine pulls the latch, eats the meat pie, and drinks the blood (Calvino, 720). In an eighteenth-century French version, the heroine unwittingly eats the flesh and drinks the blood of her grandmother (Darnton, 9-10). None of these grisly scenes appears in the modern version of the tale as collected, for example, by Andrew Lang in his *The Blue Fairy Book* (1889) (51-3).

Other grisly details of the original tales were also often removed for the sake of the new innocent readership. In the Grimms' version of "Snow White" the wicked Queen tells the huntsman: "kill her and bring me back her lungs and liver as proof of your deed." When the huntsman brings back the lungs and liver of a boar: "The cook was ordered to boil them in salt, and the wicked woman ate them and thought that she had eaten Snow White's lungs and liver" (Grimm, 197). In the first translation of the Grimms' tale by Edgar Taylor in 1823, aimed specifically at children, the Queen simply orders one of her servants to: "Take Snow-drop away into the wide wood, that I may never see her more" (Taylor, 177).

Taylor even emended some of the vengeful violence visited upon the wicked by the Brothers Grimm. At the end of the Grimms' version of "Snow White," the wicked Queen "had to put on the red-hot slippers and dance until she fell down dead" (Grimm, 204). This punishment, unseemly entertainment for a wedding, was reduced to: "she choked with passion, and fell ill and died" (Taylor, 182). The corpse of the wicked Queen can then, apparently, be conveniently removed before the wedding begins.

Interestingly, Taylor's translation of "Rumplestilskin" brings back the whimsical spirit of the original oral version. In some early versions of his tale, Rumplestilskin flies away on a spoon. By the second edition of *Household Tales*, the Grimms had written: "he stamped so violently with his right foot that his leg went deep into the ground up to his waist. Then he grabbed the other foot angrily with both hands and ripped himself in two" (Grimm, 212). In Taylor's version, the dwarf's predicament has a humorous rather than violent end. Rumplestilskin "dashed his right foot in a rage so deep into the floor, that he was forced to lay hold of it with both hands to pull it out. Then he made the best of his way off, while everybody laughed at him for having had all his trouble for nothing" (198).

The wholesale rewriting of the tales to fit with a new morality reaches its apotheosis in George Cruikshank's version of "Cinderella," where he could not forbear adding "a few Temperance Truths." When the King decrees "fountains of wine" at a celebration, Cinderella's godmother states that "the history of the use of strong drink . . . is marked on every page by excess, which follows, as a matter of course, from the very nature of their composition, and . . . always accompanied by ill-health, misery, and crime" (Tatar, *Off*, 17-8). The King is converted to teetotaling and all the beer and wine is collected for a great bonfire on the night of the wedding.

The foolishness and invasiveness of Cruikshank's additions throw all the other changes fairy tale editors made throughout the nineteenth century into bold relief. The stories had been not only emended to fit into middle-class values, but sometimes violently wrenched into propriety. And even then, despite the removal of sex and the careful focusing of violence on the wicked, that is, despite the removal of key motivations, vivid occurrences and exciting turns of the plot for the sake of the children, despite everything, the tales do not seem particularly suited to teach morals. The editors appear, in perfect hindsight, confused about what, exactly, they hoped to accomplish.

The Brothers Grimm said they hoped their work could serve as a manual of manners (Tatar, *Off*, 19). Charles Dickens writes:

It would be hard to estimate the amount of gentleness and mercy that has made its way among us through these slight channels. Forbearance, courtesy, consideration for the poor and aged, kind treatment of animals, the love of nature, abhorrence of tyranny and brute force—many such good things have been first nourished in the child's heart by this powerful aid. ("Frauds on the Fairies," 392-3)

But really, the tales are not models of good behavior, and do not teach manners or courtesy or mercy. These answers seem disingenuous, perhaps self-deceiving, although they resonate with a certain innocence in the tales, a simplicity. But that innocence belongs to the tales even in their original bawdy and violent forms. If the Brothers Grimm and Charles Dickens hoped to teach manners, a straightforward handbook would have better served. This is the position of the many children's writers who wrote "moral tales" throughout the eighteenth and nineteenth centuries, tales that *are* models of good behavior and have none of the excitement or interest, none of the imagination, of fairy tales, which is exactly the point of them. Mrs. Trimmer, an eighteenth-century educator and children's writer, comments on fairy tales:

How the heart to be cultivated by the force of imagination only, is to us inconceivable?—We are told by GOD himself, that the imagination of the heart of man is evil from his youth. (Trimmer, 208)

Mrs. Trimmer's position is diametrically opposed to the Romantic idea of childhood. Eighteenth-century educators and children's writers wrote realistic, didactic stories specifically to counter the influence of fairy tales: "Fairy tales being such dangerous fare for children, the prescribed antidote was a flood of moral tales" (Watson, "Coleridge," 21). They suppressed fairy tales or, where that proved impossible, revised them (Watson, 21). This attitude held sway throughout the eighteenth century: "This viewpoint was to produce the dreariest era in all of children's literature, and it was to last for about a hundred and fifty years" (Egoff, 24). The moral tale continued to be written throughout the nineteenth century, but children's fantasy quickly surpassed it in popularity and has outlived it on the bookshelves in the children's section of bookstores.

The fairy tale collectors who wished to convince middle-class parents to buy fairy tale collections succeeded over the moral tales, but they did not succeed by replacing one kind of moral tale for another. The tales, despite wholesale changes, remained fairy tales, imaginative works with an abiding strangeness in them. The fairy tales, that is, remained tales. The changes only allowed fantasy to adapt to its new, limited role, becoming more clearly defined as *for* children alone, which allowed it to flourish, entering the mainstream of society through the nursery door.

Chapter 3

The Moral Tale and the Fairy Tale

In the eighteenth-century, fantasy was never far away, as attested by the frequent broadsides against fairy tales from Mrs. Trimmer, John Locke (Pickering, 42-3) and others. Fantasy survived through "an effective underground movement of the literature of Romance and Faerie" (Egoff, 29). As the critic Jeanie Watson remarks in her essay, "'The Raven: A Christmas Poem'—Coleridge and the Fairy Tale Controversy," on what she calls

the imaginative world of the fabulous. It was never truly banished; instead, in the rationalistic seventeenth and eighteenth centuries, it stepped sideways, out of the mainstream of legitimate, suitable moral literature and into the "Other World" of the chapbook, in the process becoming universally available. (17)

Fantasy endured through the eighteenth century in a rich oral tradition as well (Egoff, 28). The material that had fallen under the rubric "fairy tale" by the eighteenth century included some of the oldest and most enduring works of English literature, so much so that one suspects outright suppression would have been impossible. One critic lists under eighteenth-century fairy tales:

tales from the *Gesta Romanorum* (stories mixing the myth, history, and religion of the classical Greek and Roman heroes), Aesop's *Fables, Reynard the Fox*, tales of King Arthur and his knights, Charlemagne, Robin Hood, King Horn, Valentine and Orson, Havelock the Dane, Beowulf, St. George and the Dragon, Tom Hickathrift, Guy of Warwick, and Jack the Giant-killer, as well as tales that now form the *Mabinogion*. (Egoff, 23)

A tradition of adult fairy tale material in English literature, written long before the German Romantics wrote their literary fairy tales, but in disfavor as a literary form in the eighteenth century, also ensured that fairy tales could never be completely removed from children's sight. Spenser's *The Fairie Queen* (1590-1596) and Shakespeare's *The Tempest* (1611) and *A Midsummer Night's Dream* (1595) are only the most famous examples of fairy tale-inspired poetry from the English Renaissance. A host of other original fairy works both lead up to (Darton, 93) and proceed from (Wooden, 98) Spenser and Shakespeare in the late sixteenth to mid-seventeenth century, including works by Ben Jonson and, perhaps most popular of all in its own time, Michael Drayton's *Nymphidia, The Court of Fayrie* (1627). These works drew on an older tradition, going back to mentions of fairies in Chaucer (Darton, 92) and even to far older sources (Tolkien, 129-42; Zipes, *Breaking*, 5).

In the eighteenth century itself, a fashion for fairy tales in the French court produced a number of original and collected fairy tale works that were translated and passed into England (Darton, 85), including Charles Perrault's *Histories, or Tales of Past Times, Told by Mother Goose* (1729), Countess d'Aulnoy's *Diverting Works* (1707) and other stories such as Madame de Beaumont's "Beauty and the Beast" (1756). The Arabian Nights tales, first translated into English in 1705-1708, would be translated and retranslated, imitated and revised throughout the eighteenth century (Darton, 91).

Fantasy appears so "universally available" in chapbooks, by word of mouth, in adult and foreign literature, throughout the eighteenth century, before and after, that serious questions need to be raised about how nineteenth-century children's fantasy literature marks the beginning of a "new" tradition. The writers of moral tales, unable to suppress the great wealth of fairy tale material available to children, adapt and revise much of it to their own purposes. One critic even went so far as to claim:

If one concentrates on children's literature itself rather than on the ongoing polemic in reviews and prefaces, the relation of didactic writers to the fairy tale might better be described as one of appropriation than one of censorship. (Richardson, 37)

This is an overstatement. However, the relation of didactic writers to fairy tales might be fairly characterized as one of both appropriation *and* censorship, as opposed to one of outright censorship. And, after all, the nineteenth-century collectors of fairy tales for children fare only somewhat better. The fairy tales "returned" from suppression in the nineteenth century are also altered, as the bawdy, violent "universal" tales are bowdlerized for the newly sensitive Romantic child. The return of fairy tales in the nineteenth century is indeed another appropriation, albeit one that regards fairy tales as a positive rather than a negative genre.

Children's literature, as always, written, read and bought by adults, has as much or more to do with adult notions of childhood than with children themselves. The critic Sheila Egoff correctly remarks that even works as horrific to us now as some Puritan primers, such as James Janeway's *A Token for Children, Being an Account of the Conversion, Holy and Exemplary Lives and Joyful Deaths of Several Young Children. . .* (1671), "were meant to give pleasure, the greatest pleasure that life could offer: that of going prepared and happy to God's beneficence" (25). Authors of the moral tale meant to do their best by children as well. The differences between the use of fairy tale material in the moral tale and in nineteenth-century children's fantasy literature are, while important, largely differences in ways of reading and revising the tales, not absolute differences between support or neglect of the tales.

Until relatively recently, childhood, as a unique state, did not exist (Aries, 33-4); fantasy belonged to adults and children without discrimination. After the nineteenth century, adult interest in fantasy might be considered infantile. Fantasy still belongs more to children than to adults; fantasy still remains marginal to the "great tradition" of realistic, adult works (Frye, 42-3). Fantasy's success over the moral tale, but marginal position to mainstream literature, has proven defensive and insular; fantasy has been allowed to flourish, but only within a designated and limited space, the confines of a genre. As the critic Alan Richardson notes, there is:

a dualistic model—didacticism and imagination, instruction and delight, reason and fantasy—underlying most accounts of the development of children's literature. The latter term in each opposition is, of course, invariably privileged at the expense of the former. (36)

The same model, with the opposite terms privileged, informs accounts of the moral tales presented by Mrs. Trimmer and others. The moral tale and literary fairy tale negatively required one another in order to define themselves. Moral tales are established as counter to fairy tales; nineteenth-century children's fantasy is presented as a countertradition to the moral tale. The purpose of moral tales is to expel fairy tales; the purpose of fantasy is the freedom of the imagination, but, according to its histories, freedom for children, particularly from the "dreary" moral tale.

In the argument between the moral tale and the fairy tale, fantasy's partisans write its histories and interpolate their justifications and rhetoric into the narrative of its development, uncritically celebrating fantasy's marginal status: childhood *over* adulthood, the imagination *over* reason. For example, in his history, *Children's Books in England*, Darton writes:

The history of fairy-tales and nursery rhymes, in their progress toward becoming the true natural staple of the juvenile library, is a record of strong self-preservation under neglect and deliberate persecution. (85)

Darton's work, although excellent, is written in the language of the converted: fantasy's history is a progress toward the true and the natural despite persecution. This kind of history has—in the end—had as much to say about the compromises fairy tales have had to make to survive as it has about the reasons they have prospered.

The Romantic notion that fantasy belonged to children, and to adults only when they wished to be childlike, was perhaps the most confining compromise of all because of everything it would not allow fantasy to be: literary, complex, serious. In his essay, "Frauds on the Fairies," the nineteenth-century novelist and fantasist Charles Dickens eloquently summed up this point of view in all its power and all its limitations:

> We may assume we are not singular in entertaining a very great tenderness for the fairy literature of our childhood. What enchanted us then, and is captivating a million of young fancies now, has, at the same blessed time of life, enchanted vast hosts of men and women who have done their long day's work, and laid their great heads down to rest. . . . It has greatly helped to keep us, in some sense, ever young, by preserving through our worldly ways one slender track not overgrown with weeds, where we may walk with children, sharing their delights. (392-3)

Fantasy literature as "only" a way to share delights with children is a fantasy literature, like Barrie's Peter Pan, that can never grow up.

J.R.R. Tolkien, who has been as influential as anyone in making adult fantasy commercially successful in the twentieth century, railed against the confinements of the Romantic notion that fantasy belongs exclusively to children. In his essay, "On Fairy-Stories," he writes:

> the association of children and fairy stories is an accident of our domestic history. Fairy-stories have in the modern lettered world been relegated to the "nursery," as shabby or old-fashioned furniture is relegated to the playroom, primarily because the adults do not want it, and do not mind if it is misused. (130)

Fantasy, either as "relegated" to the playroom or as the "true natural staple of the juvenile library," has had to play a role that, even if it has allowed fantasy to flourish, is nonetheless a role, and so artificial. Tolkien insists that fairy tales are not universally loved by children, nor necessarily disliked by adults, but are, rather, the taste of a particular kind of person, young or old (130).

Tolkien disagrees that fantasy and reason were opposed as well. This notion, for Tolkien, is only another instance of fantasy being treated as a literature of immaturity. Instead, Tolkien insists that fantasy is a natural human activity of adults as well as children, and that, if anything, it supports and sharpens reason. He writes:

> For creative Fantasy is founded upon the hard recognition that things are so in the world as it appears under the sun; on a recognition of fact, but not a slavery to it. So upon logic was founded the nonsense that displays itself in

the tales and rhymes of Lewis Carroll. If men really could not distinguish between frogs and men, fairy-stories about frog-kings would not have arisen. (144)

The nineteenth-century fantasist George MacDonald also insists that reason and imagination together form fantasy. MacDonald writes:

Some thinkers would feel sorely hampered if at liberty to use no forms but such as existed in nature, or to invent nothing save in accordance with the laws of the world of the senses; but it must not be therefore imagined that they desire escape from the region of law. ("Fantastic Imagination," 314)

Fantasy, Tolkien and MacDonald insist, is not a different, and by inference lesser, way of thinking, a creation of the immature, undisciplined imagination. Instead, it is an integral, even important, way of understanding and thinking about the world, on par with and a part of reason. The imagination is not in a contest with logic and law. Reality itself, they suggest, is only a blend of reason and supposition; fantasy fares no worse.

A typical history of children's fantasy begins with a quotation from the Wife of Bath about the friars chasing the fairies out of England, and ends with the fairies' inevitable and triumphant return in nineteenth-century children's fantasy. Curiously, this turn in the historical narrative imitates a narrative "turn" important to the plots of fairy tales and literary fairy tales themselves. In fairy tales, the low may be suddenly raised high, the poor man may be king, the beggar woman may prove an enchantress. Perhaps one should not be surprised if this turn was interpolated into the history of fantasy as well; and certainly fairy tales are better treated—more highly regarded as something special and important—in the nineteenth century than before. However, that should not be allowed to obscure a view of the history of the emergence of fantasy for children as yet another appropriation of fairy tales—and the new nineteenth-century genre of literary fairy tales for children—for Romantic ends, ends that both define and refine fantasy, and limit it. As the next chapter will explore, at the heart of these changes is the desire—the adult desire—not only to return to childhood, but to a divine childhood, that is, to the world of spirit itself.

Chapter 4

The Consubstantial World of Faery

In his book *Victorian Fantasy*, Prickett claims one of Romanticism's influences on the nineteenth century, and children's fantasy in particular, was "the revival of religious mysticism and a renewed feeling for the numinous—the irrational and mysterious elements in religious experience" (10-11). In nineteenth-century children's fantasy literature, the divine Romantic child showed the way to the spiritual world of fairy, a place of simple joy and revealed truth. The critic Humphrey Carpenter, in his book, *Secret Garden*, describes children's fantasy literature as the place where the adult search for an alternative spirituality could be explored. He writes:

almost without exception, the authors of the outstanding English children's books that appeared between 1860 and 1930 rejected, or had doubts about, conventional religious teaching. (13)

Carpenter believes that although these doubts are less visible in the earlier writers of children's fantasy literature, Charles Kingsley, Lewis Carroll and George MacDonald who "were all three clergymen" and had to keep "their religious uncertainties . . . beneath the surface of their writings though they were a very strong motive behind them," they become more prominent in the writings of a later group of nineteenth- and early twentieth-century children's fantasists, Kenneth Grahame,

Beatrix Potter, J.M. Barrie and A.A. Milne, who "were more conscious of their mistrust of conventional Christianity." Carpenter asserts, however, that for both groups their religious doubts inspired their fantasy, as "Their search for an Arcadia, A Good Place, a Secret Garden, was to a very large extent an attempt to find something to replace it" (13).

The most anthologized fairy tales of the nineteenth century, and the twentieth century as well, were the magical tales of transformation (many of the original tales contained no magic at all). The success of the more magical, that is, the more imaginative and transformative fairy tales, over the more realistic fairy or folk tales marked a change of values. For the late-nineteenth-century collector and buyer of fairy tales, the imagination of the heart of man, far from being evil, awakened a childhood innocence that the Romantic poets of the early nineteenth century had equated with the divine.

Coleridge read fairy tales as a child and they had a profound effect on him and his work (Watson, "Coleridge," 23). As Jeanie Watson writes in "'The Raven: A Christmas Poem'—Coleridge and the Fairy Tale Controversy":

the genre is central to "Christabel" and also makes a strong contribution to Coleridge's other well-known poems of mystery, "The Rime of the Ancient Mariner" and "Kubla Khan." The touch of faery marks lesser-known poems as well. Coleridge uses elements of the genre, or elements of what he calls "Faery," in his poetry from beginning to end. (14)

Coleridge considered fairy tales not only suitable, but significant reading for children, setting himself counter to the prevailing rationalistic notions of childhood education (Watson, 14). His position found support from "Wordsworth's denunciation of contemporary pedagogy in Book 5 of *The Prelude*" (Watson, 18). Sir Walter Scott writes of fairy tales:

there is a sort of wild fairy interest in them, which makes me think them fully better adapted to awaken the imagination and soften the heart of childhood than the good-boy stories which have been in later years composed for them. (Opie, 8)

Coleridge's daughter remarks on the suitability of fairy tales for children: "It is curious that on this point Sir Walter Scott and Charles Lamb, my father, my Uncle Southey, and Mr. Wordsworth, were all agreed" (Sara Coleridge, 137). For Coleridge and Wordsworth, as well as others in their circle, fairy tales have value because they are capable of "intensely engaging the mind" (Watson, 14), opening up the imagination to other worlds of experience.

In his letters, Coleridge writes of being an eight-year-old boy listening "on a winter evening" to his father talk about the planets and constellations:

> I heard him with a profound delight & admiration; but without the least mixture of wonder or incredulity. For from my early reading of Faery Tales, & Genii &c &c—my mind has been habituated to the Vast—& I never regarded my senses in any way as the criteria of my belief. I regulated all my creeds by my conceptions not by my sight—even at that age. (*The Collected Letters*, 1: 354)

In *The Prelude*, Wordsworth remarks, in a similar vein, on why, as a boy, he felt no fear at the sight of a dead body raised suddenly from Esthwaite's Lake:

> for my inner eye had seen
> Such sights before among the shining streams
> Of faery land, the forests of romance. (5: 475-7)

Wordsworth's imagination has been prepared not only for the wondrous, such as the sight of the stars, but for the strange and shocking.

Fairy tales, according to Wordsworth and Coleridge, could raise children up out of contemplation of the world, and allow them to realize something stranger and perhaps greater. Coleridge continues in his letters:

> Should children be permitted to read Romances, & Relations of Giants & Magicians, & Genii?—I know all that has been said against it; but I have formed my faith in the affirmative.—I know no other way of giving the mind a love of "the Great," & "the Whole."—Those who have been led to the same truths step by step thro' the constant testimony of their senses, seem to me to want a sense which I possess—They contemplate nothing but parts—and all parts are necessarily little—and the Universe to them is but a

mass of little things.—It is true, that the mind may become credulous & prone to superstition by the former method—but are not the Experimentalists credulous even to madness in believing any absurdity, rather than believe the grandest truths, if they have not the testimony of their own senses in their favor?—I have known some who have been rationally educated, as it is styled. They were marked by a microscopic acuteness; but when they looked at great things, all became a blank & they saw nothing—and denied (very illogically) that any thing could be seen: and uniformly put the negation of a power for the possession of power—& called the Want of imagination Judgement, & the never being moved to Rapture Philosophy. (1: 354-5)

Fairy tales, through the engagement of the imagination, may move the reader toward rapture and toward apprehension of the unity of all things.

Jeanie Watson describes fairy tales as a representation for Coleridge of the consubstantial world, reconciling humanity's spiritual and material existence:

The consubstantial world is a symbolic world in which spirit manifests its being as the ongoing reconciliation of polarities in the things of this world, and the things of this world—whether the process and forms of nature or the human soul or the creative imagination—simultaneously represent and participate in the One Life that is Spirit. The realm of Faery becomes a symbolic metaphor for Spirit/God/the One Life, and the tale of Faery shows forth that Reality. Within this context, the tale of Faery may be more profoundly 'moral' than the moral tale because it leads to the spiritual truths upon which morality is based. ("Coleridge," 15)

For Coleridge, fairy tales had a moral purpose—a deeper purpose than even overtly moralistic tales—since they led to the world of the spirit. Fairy tales for children had an educational function as clearly as eighteenth-century moral tales did, and they had a spiritual function as well. They could not improve the Romantic child, more perfect than any faded adult, but they might awaken the imagination and rouse the spirit to a remembrance and realization of the glory clinging to us yet "From God, who is our home" (Wordsworth, "Ode," line 65).

The Victorian fantasy writer G.K. Chesterson, in his essay, "Fairy Tales" (1908), wittily explains the essential morality of traditional fairy tales, and so of fantasy and the imagination:

Some solemn and superficial people (for nearly all superficial people are solemn) have declared that the fairy tales are immoral; they base this upon some accidental circumstances or regrettable incidents in the war between giants and boys, some cases in which the latter indulged in unsympathetic deceptions or even in practical jokes. The objection, however, is not only false, but very much the reverse of the facts. The fairy tales are at root not only moral in the sense of being innocent, but moral in the sense of being didactic, moral in the sense of being moralising. (253)

Later in his essay, Chesterson goes on to explain:

If you really read the fairy-tales, you will observe that one idea runs from one end of them to the other—the idea that peace and happiness can only exist on some condition. This idea, which is the core of ethics, is the core of nursery-tales. The whole happiness of fairyland hangs on a thread, upon one thread. Cinderella may have a dress woven on supernatural looms and blazing with unearthly brilliance; but she must be back when the clock strikes twelve. The King may invite fairies to the christening, but he must invite all the fairies or frightful results will follow. Bluebeard's wife may open all doors but one. A promise is broken to a cat, and the whole world goes wrong. A promise is broken to a yellow dwarf, and the whole world goes wrong. A girl may be the bride of the God of Love himself if she never tries to see him; she sees him, and he vanishes away. A girl is given a box on condition she does not open it; she opens it, and all the evils of this world rush out at her. A man and a woman are put in a garden on condition that they do not eat one fruit: they eat it, and lose their joy in all fruits of the earth. (255-6)

Chesterson suggests that humanity's fall from Eden was a fall from a fairyland world of the spirit into the "real" world we know. Fairy tales, fantasy, through the innocence of the imagination, can recover the moral world of grace before the fall. Chesterson writes:

This is the profound morality of fairy tales; which so far from being lawless, go to the root of all law. Instead of finding (like common books of ethics) a rationalistic basis for each Commandment, they find the great mystical basis for all Commandments. (257)

Fantasy for Chesterson, as for Coleridge, rises above the details of the world in order to see, through the grace of the imagination, the great and the whole; and once the imagination apprehends the whole world as one, then the numinous world, the consubstantial world, the moral world of the spirit, opens up and takes one into the sublime.

Twentieth-century fantasist C.S. Lewis writes of the power of literary fantasy to arouse in the reader a desire for something beyond, and perhaps far greater:

> It stirs and troubles him (to his life-long enrichment) with the dim sense of something beyond his reach and far, far from dulling or emptying the actual world, gives it new dimension of depth. He does not despise real woods because he has read of enchanted woods: the reading makes all real woods a little enchanted. ("On Three Ways of Writing For Children," 38)

The great nineteenth-century writer of children's fairy tales, George MacDonald, describes fantasy's rousing of the imagination in an essay on "The Fantastic Imagination," explicitly linking it to the soul:

> If a writer's aim be logical conviction, he must spare no logical pains, not merely to be understood, but to escape being misunderstood; where his object is to move by suggestion, to cause to imagine, then let him assail the soul of his reader as the wind assails an aeolian harp. If there be music in my reader, I would gladly wake it. Let fairytale of mine go for a firefly that now flashes, now is dark, but may flash again. Caught in a hand which does not love its kind, it will turn to an insignificant, ugly thing, that can neither flash nor fly. (321)

The reader's imagination must be inspired for fantasy to be effective. Fantastic stories, in and of themselves, fail unless they suggest something more, something greater beyond the text, and this something greater resides for MacDonald in the soul.

In his essay "On Fairy-Stories," Tolkien defined fairy stories not by the presence of fairies, but rather the presence of *Faerie,* of another world, unreachable within the text itself:

> The definition of a fairy-story—what it is, or what it should be—does not, then, depend on any definition or historical account of elf or fairy, but upon the nature of *Faerie*: the Perilous Realm itself, and the air that blows in that country. I will not attempt to define that, nor describe it directly. It cannot be done. *Faerie* cannot be caught in a net of words; for it is one of its

qualities to be indescribable, though not imperceptible. (114)

Both MacDonald and Tolkien speak of fantasy as a wind that blows from beyond the world, a typical Romantic metaphor for describing an overflow of feeling moving through the soul (Abrams, 26). Fantasy itself cannot reveal this other world; it can only bring the reader to the moment of perception before apprehension of it, that is, to the moment of the expression of its quality of being "indescribable, though not imperceptible." Fantasy can bring the reader right to the edge of the primeval forest that is so often the border of fairyland in fairy tales. But the reader must step inside alone. This movement beyond the actual requires the active participation of the reader's "willing suspension of disbelief . . . which constitutes poetic faith" (Coleridge, *Biographia*, 2:6), just as religious rapture requires the subject's belief as a necessary step.

This kind of fantasy, Tolkien's fairy story, requires the subject to, as Wordsworth said, "see into the life of things," as Wilde's Selfish Giant saw the little boy for who he truly was—the Christ child. This movement beyond the text is a fundamental element of literary fairy stories and the Romantic way of reading fairy tales. As Iona and Peter Opie explicate "Cinderella":

The prince's admiration of her in her party dress is worthless. It is essential he plights himself to her while she is a kitchen maid, or the spell can never be broken. (14)

This kind of breaking of the spell, which requires one to see the truth with the magic eyes of the imagination, has, as the Opies point out, "a curious parallel to the Christ story." Christ, the divine made flesh, must be accepted in his humble state as a simple carpenter; he may not reveal himself in his glory even when mocked and put to death for "Had Christ been shown in his full glory, recognition of his virtues, whether by pauper or by prince, would have been valueless." When Cinderella is recognized as pure at heart, just as when Christ is recognized as the divine made flesh, the recognition

is not an actual transformation but a disenchantment, the breaking of a spell. In each case we are aware that the person was always noble, that the magic has wrought no change in the person's soul, only in his or her outward form. In fairy tales there is no saving of the wicked heart. (Opie, 14)

The transformation of fairy tales by fairy tale collectors in the nineteenth century is also not an actual transformation, but the breaking of a spell. The stories, in their original state as simple oral tales, had been powerful expressions of the imagination. Romanticism changed how readers read fairy tales. For the Romantics, especially Coleridge, fairy tales and fairy stories engaged the heart, opening the reader to the experience of the world of the spirit; for the Romantics, especially Wordsworth, childhood expressed the presence of the glory of heaven. For both, the act of imagining is a movement toward the world of spirit. In the nineteenth century, childhood became the time and fantasy the place of the divine.

The nineteenth-century fantasy writer Francis Browne, in her fine fantasy *Granny's Wonderful Chair* (1856), also reads the loss of fairyland as a fall from grace, and suggests the possibility of redemption through the imagination, the possibility that fantastic stories might sweep one up again into the world of the spirit. At the end of her collection of fairy tales, each beginning with the wonderfully evocative formula, "Chair of my Grandmother, tell me a story," the narrator comments of fairy:

that time is long ago. Great wars, work and learning have passed over the world since then and altered all its fashions. Kings make no seven-day feasts for all comers now. . . . Chairs tell no tales. Wells work no wonders; and there are no such doings on hills and forests, for the fairies dance no more. Some say it was the hum of schools—some think it was the din of factories that frightened them; but nobody has been known to have seen them for many a year, except, it is said, one Hans Christian Andersen, in Denmark, whose tales of the fairies are so good that they must have been heard from themselves.

It is certain no living man knows the subsequent history of King Winwealth's country, nor what became of the notable characters who lived and visited his palace. Yet there are people who believe . . . that Dame Frostyface yet spins—they cannot tell where; that Snowflower may yet be seen at the new year's time in her dress of white velvet, looking out for the early spring; that Prince Wisewit has somehow fallen under a stronger spell and a thicker cushion, that he still tells stories to Snowflower and her friends, and when both cushion and spell are broken by another stroke of Sturdy's hatchet—which they expect will happen some time—the prince will make all things right again, and bring the fairy times to the world. (126-7)

Fantastic stories have often been a way to realize the spiritual world, both in myths and in literature, in works like Dante's *Commedia* (ca. 1300), Spenser's *Faerie Queen* (1590-1611), Milton's *Paradise Lost* (1667) and Bunyan's *Pilgrim's Progress* (1678-1684). In the mid- to late-nineteenth-century, children's fantasy literature continued that tradition, albeit outside the mainstream of literature, in the form indicated and the structure outlined by Romanticism at the beginning of the century. In Part II, this work will compare the structure of transcendence in Romantic poetry—the natural sublime—to specific works of nineteenth-century fantasy literature for children, outlining the structure of the fantastic sublime.

PART II

THE WIND FROM BEYOND THE WORLD

Chapter 5

The "Correspondent Breeze"

M.H. Abrams observes that as earlier poets invoked the muse, or the Holy Spirit, for inspiration, the Romantics called upon the wind. The wind brought spring, life from a dead land, the return of creativity and the renewal of faith (26). Often it served as a Romantic metaphor for the unseen presence of the world of the spirit. William Wordsworth opens his greatest poem, *The Prelude*: "Oh there is blessing in this gentle breeze. . ." (I: 1). This blessing breeze, "the breath of heaven" (33), would later act "Spontaneously to clothe in priestly robe/ A renovated spirit singled out/ . . . for holy services" (1:52-4). Samuel Taylor Coleridge writes of a mystic wind in his letters, describing how as

a traveller up on an alpine road . . . my spirit courses, drives and eddies, like a Leaf in Autumn: a wild activity, of thoughts, imaginations, feelings, and impulses of motion, rises up from within me—a sort of *bottom-wind,* that blows to no point of the compass, & comes from I know not whence, but agitates the whole of me. . . . Life seems to me then a universal spirit. (*The Collected Letters*, 14 January, 1803; 2: 916)

In Romantic form, Kenneth Grahame's *The Wind in the Willows* and George MacDonald's *At the Back of the North Wind* begin with just such mystic bottom winds.

In *The Wind in the Willows*, Mole is roused by "Spring . . . moving in the air and in the earth below and around him, penetrating even his dark and lowly little house with its spirit of divine discontent and longing." He knew suddenly, "Something up above was calling him imperiously" (ch. 1; 1). Wordsworth writes of "Spontaneous wisdom," how "One impulse from a vernal wood/ May teach you more of man/ Of moral evil and of good,/ than all the sages can" ("Tables Turned," 21-4). Such an impulse, natural and joyous, calls Mole out from his pent-up existence whitewashing his little home to "the joy of living and the delight of spring without its cleaning" (ch. 1; 2). In *The Prelude*, Wordsworth writes how "the soft breeze can come/ To none more grateful than to me; escaped/ From the vast city" (I: 5-7). Mole is also escaped (from his whitewashing), also a renovated spirit, called to holy service; he leaps and laughs and bowls past others who do not see the glory he sees in nature that day.

Specifically, Mole is called out to life on what his friend Rat calls "*The* River" (ch. 1; 9). The River is like an always open holy book—"a babbling procession of the best stories in the world, sent from the heart of the earth to be told at last to the insatiable sea" (ch. 1; 4). Full of surprises and ecstatic energy, The River is described as enchanting, bewitching, fascinating, intoxicating, dreamy. Mole immediately takes up the Romantic pastime of "messing about in boats" (7), where "intoxicated with the sparkle, the ripple, the scents and the sounds and the sunlight, he trailed a paw in the water and dreamed long waking dreams" (ch. 1; 9). He becomes immediately a Romantic dreamer in pursuit of aesthetic rapture.

In an essay, "Loafing," Grahame expands on the ecstatic joys of the Romantic idler "messing about in boats":

With one paddle out he will drift down the stream: just brushing the flowering rush and the meadow sweet and taking in as peculiar gifts the varied sweets of even. The loosestrife is his, and the arrow-head: his the distant moan of the weir; his are the glories, amber and scarlet and silver, of the sunset-haunted surface. By-and-by the boaters will pass him homeward-bound. All are blistered and sore: his withers are unwrung. Most are too tired and hungry to see the sunset glories; no corporeal pangs clog his æsthesis—his perceptive faculty. Some have quarreled in the day and are no longer on speaking terms; he is at peace with himself and with the whole world. (*The Pagan Papers*, 52)

Similarly, in his poem, "Frost at Midnight," Coleridge writes of his wish that his infant son, when he becomes a boy, might

> wander like a breeze
> By lakes and sandy shores. . . .
> so shalt thou see and hear
> The lovely shapes and sounds intelligible
> Of that eternal language, Which thy God
> Utters, who from eternity doth teach
> Himself in all, and all things in himself. (54-62)

Idling by the riverbank, Mole hears such an eternal language uttered by a divine agent as "with his ears to the reed-streams he caught, at intervals, something of what the wind went whispering so constantly among them" (ch. 1; 22). On the river lies a sacred island inhabited by the nature god, Pan, whose mystic music whispers in the willows, inviting and instructing.

As the wind replaced the muse, so the poetic "lyre of Apollo was often replaced in Romantic poetry by the Æolian lyre, whose music is evoked not by art, human or divine, but by a force of nature" (Abrams, 26). In Romantic poetry, the Æolian lyre, or wind-harp, provided a figure for what Wordsworth calls the "correspondent breeze" (*Prelude*, I, 35), the mediation "between outer motion and inner emotion" (Abrams, 26), that is, the correspondence between the inner and outer life or (in what may be the same thing) between the outer world and beyond, the transcendent. A Romantic wind from beyond the world blows through *The Wind in the Willows* and the willows act as an Æolian lyre, a correspondent breeze, leading toward an apprehension of the sacred in nature.

In George MacDonald's *At the Back of the North Wind*, Diamond is awakened by a persistent voice whispering in the wind demanding to be let in. Wordsworth writes how: "Visionary power/ Attends the motions of the viewless winds" (*Prelude*, V, 595-6). In MacDonald's work, the visionary wind, the song of the Æolian lyre itself, appears as an actual presence named North Wind. North Wind, talking to Diamond through "the piece of paper his mother had posted over the hole" (ch. 1; 10) in the wall of his hayloft bedroom, demands Diamond reopen what she calls "my window" (11). Diamond refuses because the cold wind might "give me the toothache" (12). But the wind will not relent:

You shall not be the worse for it, I promise you that. You shall be much better for it. Just you believe what I say, and do as I tell you. (12)

Diamond does as he is told and peels off the paper; and like the simple heroes of old fairy tales who are rewarded beyond measure just for listening to the peculiar advice of the talking fox, the whispering willow or the old healer woman, Diamond listens to the magic voice and gains a spirit helper and guide. The wind rushes in, and though Diamond hides beneath his bedclothes, the world of the spirit, once invited, overwhelms and sweeps one up into the transcendent.

"Will you take your head out of the bedclothes?" said the voice, just a little angrily.
"No!" answered Diamond, half peevish, half frightened.
The instant he said the word, a tremendous blast of wind crashed in the board of the wall, and swept the clothes off Diamond. He started up in terror. Leaning over him was the large, beautiful, pale face of a woman. Her dark eyes looked a little angry, for they had just begun to flash; but a quivering in her sweet upper lip made her look as if she were going to cry. What was most strange was that away from her head streamed out her black hair in every direction, so that the darkness in the hay-loft looked as if it were made of her hair; but as Diamond gazed at her in speechless amazement, mingled with confidence—for the boy was entranced with her mighty beauty—her hair began to gather itself out of the darkness, and fell down all about her again, till her face looked out from the midst of it like a moon out of a cloud. From her eyes came the light by which Diamond saw her face and her hair. (14-5)

The mystical, goddesslike figure of North Wind takes Diamond flying, held in her arms or tangled in her infinite hair. She tells Diamond of the land at the back of the north wind and of a "far off song" (ch. 7; 65-6) she hears from there, which promises a coming end to all suffering. Eventually, Diamond asks and she takes him back of the north wind, into the world of spirit itself.

A Romantic wind from beyond the world blows through *At the Back of the North Wind* as through *The Wind in the Willows*.

Diamond, like Mole, is roused by the visionary Romantic wind made actual through the presence, or negative presence, of a fantastic figure: for Diamond, North Wind; for Mole, Pan. North Wind's far-off song sounds another correspondent breeze, like the pipes of pan sounding in the willows, leading toward the apprehension of the sacred in nature.

Chapter 6

From the Romantic to the Fantastic Sublime

In Romanticism, the apprehension of the spirit in nature has been called the "natural sublime." In the sublime moment, the contemplation of a natural object leads to an aesthetic rapture, which produces a correspondent overflow of feeling, revealing the transcendent. In "Tintern Abbey," Wordsworth describes "a sense sublime/ Of something far more deeply interfused. . . . A motion and a spirit that impels/ All thinking things, all objects of all thoughts,/ and rolls through all things" (95-102). Coleridge calls it the experience of "the one Life within us and abroad,/ Which meets all motion and becomes its soul" ("Eolian Harp," 26-7), the great movement of something, not the self, which exists without and within, sweeping the self away in a unity of this world and the world of the spirit.

Coleridge presents as an example of the sublime "A Mountain in a cloudless sky, its summit . . . hidden by clouds and seemingly blended with the sky, while mists and floating vapors encompass it, is sublime" (Shawcross, 342). For Coleridge, a natural object, to engender the sublime, must have an incomplete quality that paradoxically leads the mind to seek for more. It must be suggestive of infinity. Raimonda Modiano writes:

for Coleridge the essential qualities which occasion the sublime are boundlessness and indefiniteness. Yet Coleridge's emphasis is not so much on infinite extension as on the quality of perceptual indistinctness which allows certain objects to lose their individual form and blend with one another into a whole, though not one that can be grasped fully. (115)

The hidden mountain blending with the sky implies more than mountain and sky, a completeness and wholeness of the world. It implies the consubstantial world, the one life of the spirit. For Coleridge, "the lack of distinct boundaries and spatial specificity serves as the means of conveying to the mind an impression of unity" (115). Where the mountain uncovered would be merely "Grand" or "Majestic," the hidden summit is "Sublime" (Modiano, 114).

Wordsworth describes the natural sublime as "dwelling in the light of setting suns,/ And the round ocean and the living air,/ And the blue sky, and in the mind of man" ("Tintern Abbey," 97-9). The setting sun, half-faded into night, the round ocean, disappearing over the horizon, the living air, the wind blowing from beyond the world, are Romantic images of loss, of what cannot be fully known. No natural object in itself is sublime. The mind, suddenly free from the phenomenal through indefiniteness and suggestiveness, experiences the sublime. The sublime is centered in subject not object, in a dissolution into unity that reveals an absolute essence to the mind.

MacDonald describes the effect of fantasy literature with images recalling Coleridge's misty mountaintop and Wordsworth's setting sun: "A fairytale, a sonata, a gathering storm, a limitless night, seizes you and sweeps you away" ("Fantastic Imagination," 319). In both Romantic poetry and fantastic literature, the imagination reaches beyond its grasp in a movement towards transcendence.

The critic Thomas Weiskel suggests that the sublime in Romantic poetry replaced, or at least attempted to replace, earlier methods of transcendence, whether religious or otherwise:

The Romantic sublime was an attempt to revise the meaning of transcendence precisely when the traditional apparatus of sublimation—spiritual, ontological, and (one gathers) psychological, and even perceptual—was failing to be exercised or understood. (4)

Neil Hertz also links the religious and the sublime, saying it draws much of its power from the literature of religious conversion, that is, from a literature that describes major experiential transformation, the mind not merely challenged and thereby invigorated but thoroughly "turned around." (47)

The mind is "turned around" in religious conversion to belief, to acceptance of the world of the spirit, and the Romantic sublime promises such an experiential "turn."

The fantastic also lies close to religious experience. After all, fantastic stories, as myth, that is, as accepted truth, have explored the world of the spirit perhaps since the beginning of story. The critic Andras Sandor remarks on the affinity of the religious and the fantastic in his essay on "Myths and the Fantastic":

The space left empty by the withdrawal of myths under the onslaught of Enlightenment has been filled with stories, and the stories which have so far been the closest to myths are fantastic stories. (339)

Through the construction of the fantastic sublime, this work will attempt to describe fantasy's peculiar affinity with what Hertz called "major experiential transformation," with the literature of religious conversion as interpreted by the Romantic notion of the natural sublime.

Weiskel describes the sublime as beginning with a contemplated object that is considered sublime when "the attempt to represent it determines the mind to regard its inability to grasp wholly the object as a symbol of the mind's relation to a transcendent order" (23). In his journals, Weiskel writes: "I see now—this will be the working definition of the sublime—it is that moment when the relation between the signifier and signified breaks down and is replaced by an indeterminate relationship" (qtd. in Portia Williams Weiskel, ix). The sublime, like fantasy, requires a grasping beyond the actual, beyond what is known, or can be known, of something, that is, the relation between signifier and signified, a reach exceeding grasp which promises the transcendent beyond.

Weiskel describes the structure of the sublime as divided into three stages. In the first phase, the mind is in a determinate, habitual relationship with the contemplated object. In the second phase, in an overflow of feeling,

the habitual relation of mind and object suddenly breaks down. Surprise and astonishment is the affective correlative, and there is an immediate intuition of a disconcerting disproportion between inner and outer. Either mind or object is suddenly in excess—and then both are since their relation has become radically indeterminate. In the third, or reactive, phase of the sublime moment, the mind recovers the balance of outer and inner by constituting a fresh relation between itself and the object such that the very indeterminacy which erupted in phase two is taken as symbolizing the mind's relation to a transcendent order. (23-4)

The second phase is experienced as the tearing of a veil between this world and another field of experience altogether, one both more immediate and more intense. Paradoxically, the transcendence of the sublime, although centered in the subject, requires, in order to reach through the veil to the moment of unity, a self-effacement, a loss of the self.

This loss, which might be regarded as a kind of freeing of the self, is expressed in Romanticism through two distinct kinds of forgetfulness, or rather, two distinct states of being—the world and the world of spirit—each requiring one to forget about the other state. First, an a priori, or in-born, forgetfulness of the world of the spirit out of which one came into existence, makes the experience of the second phase of the sublime a revelation of sudden remembrance, the dropping of an amnesia, the return of something lost. In "Ode: Intimations of Immortality," Wordsworth writes: "Our birth is but a sleep and a forgetting," but he describes something that yet abides, some trace memory: "Not in entire forgetfulness,/ And not in utter nakedness,/ But trailing clouds of glory do we come/ From God, who is our home" (58-65).

The trace memory of glory, strongest in unselfconscious childhood, leads to a longing for the lost world of the spirit and, ironically, in the very movement toward spirit, to the second kind of forgetfulness. In the second kind of forgetfulness expressed in Romanticism, the forgetfulness of the sublime moment, we must forget what we have become in this world in order to remember the glory of our once and future home in spirit. Wordsworth dramatizes the transcendence of self in *The Prelude* as "spots of time" (12: 208), indeterminate moments when time and place and person loosen their hold on the individual in epiphanies of childhood imaginative experience.

Self-forgetfulness is also important in children's fantasy, and is the other side of Wordsworth's and Coleridge's claims that fairy tales "habituated" the mind to the vast and the whole. In order to move toward the vast, the narrow confines of the self must be left behind in flights of imagination and fantasy. In *The Prelude*, Wordsworth writes:

> Oh! give us once again the wishing cap
> Of Fortunatus, and the invisible coat
> Of Jack the Giant-killer, Robin Hood
> And Sabra in the forest of St. George!
> The child whose love is here, at least, doth reap
> One precious gain, that he forget himself. (5: 341-6)

Coleridge, in a defense of fairy and adventure tales, writes of children's fantasy literature:

Nothing should be more impressed on parents and tutors than to make children forget themselves; and books which only told how Master Billy and Miss Ann spoke and acted were not only ridiculous but extremely harmful. Much better to give them "Jack-the-Giant-Killer" or the "Seven Champions" or anything, which being their sphere of action, should not feed self-pride. (*Shakespearean Criticism*, 2: 292)

For Wordsworth and Coleridge, realistic children's stories only serve to make children acutely self-conscious and prideful. It is better to release them into fairy tales and the imagination, into dreams of other worlds, and closer to the remembrance of the glory of the world of the spirit.

Northrop Frye discusses self-forgetfulness in fantasy literature in general:

Whether romance begins with a hero whose birth is, as Wordsworth says, a sleep and a forgetting, or whether it begins with a sinking from a waking world into a dream world, it is logical for it to begin its series of adventures with some kind of break in consciousness, one which often involves actual forgetfulness of the previous state. We may call this the motif of amnesia. (102)

The loss of self is not without dangers, however. Frye describes fantasy's "break in consciousness," such as "wandering into the land of fairies," as "involving a change so drastic as to give the sense of becoming someone else altogether" (103). Frye states: "the structural core [of fantasy] is the individual loss or confusion or break in the continuity of identity" (104). Fantasy can occasion an intense, frightening breakdown of identity, a breakdown that leads to another world, the world of dreams and imagination, and of spirit.

This breakdown is characteristic of the second phase of the sublime moment. While necessary to the recovery of the third phase, it also holds real danger, sometimes called the "blockage of the sublime." Weiskel describes "an abridgement of the sublime moment so that we are confined to the second phase and await futilely the restorative reaction which never comes, except ironically" (26). In this abridgement of the sublime, the tearing of the veil becomes an endless tearing, an opening without end or release, where the third or restorative phase never comes. Morris describes the sublime as:

an experience in which words and images grow radically unstable, where meaning is continually in question, approaching or receding or fixed on a distant horizon, promising new dimensions of insight or (in abrupt absences) unexpectedly blocking the mind. ("Gothic Sublimity," 299)

Neil Hertz put forward Wordsworth's Simplon Pass episode and the encounter with the Blind Beggar from *The Prelude* as examples of the blockage of the sublime (44). In each example, Wordsworth is lost and confused and his visionary moment ends not in transcendence but in letdown and disappointment. The sublime moment risks the subject's sense of identity in a bewildering moment of uncertainty that may lead only to more bafflement.

In his paper on the fantastic, "The Uncanny" (1919)—which Harold Bloom calls "Freud's theory of the sublime" ("Freud," 218)—Sigmund Freud describes a kind of blockage in fantasy literature as taking part in the confusion of the German words *heimlich* and *unheimlich*, "canny" and "uncanny," which through common usage merge and come to mean their opposites (377). In this move, the supernatural is found to be the natural, the other is distressingly discovered to be the self, that is, the *unheimlich* is *heimlich*. This ownership proves claustrophobic, for what comes hidden in the guise of the fantastic turns out to be the inferior term in the self's production of itself, the repressed unconscious (389-94). Morris writes:

> For Freud, the uncanny derives its terror not from something external, alien or unknown but—on the contrary—from something strangely familiar which defeats our efforts to separate ourselves from it. ("Gothic Sublimity," 307)

In the uncanny moment, the radical otherness of fantasy is experienced as a challenge to one's construction of reality and a subversion of one's understanding of self.

In nineteenth-century fantasy literature, the blockage of the sublime marks the Gothic, what Freud calls the "uncanny," the literature of fear. The transcendent sublime, where the second phase gives way to the third, bringing release and restoration, marks what Tolkien calls fairy stories and describes much nineteenth-century children's fantasy, what might be called the "literature of joy." Nineteenth-century Gothic literature fragments and collapses, as in Poe's "The Fall of the House of Usher" (1840), Stevenson's *Dr. Jekyll and Mr. Hyde* (1886) or Wilde's *The Picture of Dorian Gray* (1891). Nineteenth-century children's fantasy literature, presided over by the divine child, moves outward on a visionary journey and return, on a quest toward the transcendent and spiritual. However, the risk of blockage, of the confusion of identity, of feelings of loss and abandonment, plays an important role in fairy stories as a necessary precursor to a sudden release.

Through the psychological breakdown of the uncanny, fantasy takes part in the overwhelming of the senses by the sublime, the rush of feeling leading to self-effacement where the self and not-self are suddenly out of balance. In fairy stories, unlike the Gothic, this leads to the next step of the sublime: the apprehension and awe of the oneness of everything. In fairy stories, as in the natural sublime, the breakdown of the imagination becomes less a failure than a method for the self to loosen itself, through crisis, from the constraints of reason, consciousness, society—whatever is known, defined, explained.

According to Tolkien in his landmark essay "On Fairy-Stories," fantasy literature—fairy stories—through the action of "arresting strangeness" (156), offers three distinct gifts: Recovery, Escape and

Consolation. These three gifts have a kinship to the three phases of the sublime moment.

In Recovery, as the critic Jack Zipes observes, "The placing of objects from our everyday world in a luminous, estranged setting compels us to perceive them in a new way" (*Breaking*, 143). Tolkien carefully explains that he would not describe Recovery as revealing things in essence or truth, only claiming that he might call it "seeing things as we are (or were) meant to see them," freed from "familiarity—from possessiveness" (165). Recovery is the tearing of the veil between worlds, an apprehension of the otherness of things, the movement into the second phase of the sublime. The self-effacement of the sublime, the leaving behind of the cares of this world, is evident in the shedding of possessiveness.

Escape also provides a loosening of the constraints of the world characteristic of the self-effacement of the second phase of the sublime moment. Tolkien does not mean Escape in a negative sense, writing that it might be "practical," or even "heroic" (173), as it strives to leave behind all the cares and sorrows of the world in pursuit of the gift of Consolation, the joy and restoration of the third phase of the sublime.

Finally, Consolation is the release and transcendence of fairy stories, which in one of its aspects, the happy ending, Tolkien calls" eucatastrophe." In "On Fairy-Stories," he defines eucatastrophe as:

a sudden and miraculous grace: never to be counted on to recur. It does not deny the existence of dyscatastrophe, of sorrow and failure: the possibility of these is necessary to the joy of deliverance; it denies (in the face of much evidence, if you will) universal final defeat and in so far is *evangelium*, giving a fleeting glimpse of Joy, Joy beyond the walls of the world, poignant as grief. (153)

Tolkien's Consolation is the fantastic sublime, drawn from the Romantic tradition of the natural sublime, both extending and revising it.

This kind of fantastic literature, Tolkien's fairy story, is a transformational literature, focused, like Romanticism, on the individual, on the spiritual, on the imagination. The fantastic sublime must move the reader to glimpse beyond the printed page, because the sublime does not lie in the text at all, but reveals, beyond it, Joy, with a capital J. The fantastic sublime, like the natural sublime, requires a visionary to arouse wonder and desire, fear of loss of identity and a sudden rising above that is "poignant as grief." Only a certain kind of reader, bringing longing and a shaping spirit of imagination, will find the sublime in the fantastic text at all.

Lewis Carroll's *Alice in Wonderland* provides examples of both the blockage and the consolation of the fantastic sublime. The emphasis of Carroll's nonsense on confusion and bewilderment may lead one to regard *Alice* as interested almost exclusively in the blockage of the sublime. However, this point of view fails to realize that the fear in Carroll's book, while real, is less than the silliness in it and underestimates the strength of Alice's character in resisting attempts to baffle or alarm her. Nevertheless, Northrop Frye points out the disturbing elusiveness of the fantasy in *Alice*:

Alice is always either too big or too small, hence often a nuisance or an unwanted guest. She feels estranged from her body by changes in size, and falls into a pool of what a post-Victorian reader would simply call her liquid excretions. A sinister beheading queen makes her appearance, and the theme of metamorphosis is introduced in the witches' kitchen of the ugly duchess, where a little boy turns into a pig. . . . The story ends in a trial in which all the characters present turn on the heroine. We notice the prominence of cards in the story; cards and dice are common in descent narratives, because of their overtones of fatality and chance. (124)

However, Alice also experienced, in a moment of calm, the unity of all things when she stepped into a forest of forgetfulness, into the fantastic sublime:

Just then a Fawn came wandering by: it looked at Alice with its large gentle eyes, but didn't seem at all frightened. "Here then! Here then!" Alice said, as she held out her hand and tried to stroke it; but it only started a little, and then stood looking at her again.

"What do you call yourself?" the Fawn said at last. Such a soft sweet voice it had!

"I wish I knew!" thought poor Alice. She answered, rather sadly, "Nothing, just now."

"Think again," it said: "that won't do."

Alice thought, but nothing came of it. "Please, would you tell me what *you* call yourself?" she said timidly. "I think that might help a little."

"I'll tell you, if you'll come a little further on," the fawn said. "I can't remember *here*."

So they walked on together through the wood, Alice with her arms clasped lovingly round the soft neck of the Fawn, till they came out into another open field, and here the Fawn gave a sudden bound into the air, and shook itself free from Alice's arm. "I'm a Fawn!" it cried out in a voice of delight. "And, dear me! you're a human child!" A sudden look of alarm came into its beautiful brown eyes, and in another moment it had darted away at full speed. (226-7)

The difference between the forest of forgetfulness, the world without names or fear, and the world of language, the prison of place and self, is the difference between the self in the world and the sublime move beyond the world. Martin Gardner comments on this passage:

The wood in which things have no name is in fact the universe itself, as it is apart from symbol-manipulating creatures who label portions of it because—as Alice earlier remarked with pragmatic wisdom—"it's useful to the people that name them." The realization that the world by itself contains no signs—that there is no connection whatever between things and their names except by way of a mind that finds the tags useful—is by no means a trivial philosophic insight. (227)

Beyond the breakdown of the relationship between signified and signifier, the sublime dissolves all into the consubstantial world where the lion may lay down with the lamb, or a child walk with a fawn.

The use of the forest, of nature, to represent spiritual harmony is characteristic of nineteenth-century children's fantasy just as it is characteristic of Romantic poetry. Wordsworthian nature acts as a spiritual guide: "Let Nature be your Teacher," ("The Tables Turned," 16), as Wordsworth writes. MacDonald describes the connection between nature and the fantastic in Wordsworthian terms:

The best Nature does for us is to work in us such moods in which thoughts of high import arise. Does any aspect of Nature wake but one thought? Does she ever suggest only one definite thing? Does she make any two men in the same place at the same moment think the same thing? Is she therefore a failure, because she is not definite? Is it nothing that she rouses the something deeper than understanding—the power that underlies thoughts? Does she not set feeling, and so thinking at work? Would it be better that she did this after one fashion and not after many fashions? Nature is mood-engendering, thought-provoking: such ought the sonata, such ought the fairytale to be. (MacDonald, "The Fantastic Imagination," 19)

For MacDonald, the experience of a fairy tale, like the experience of nature, could lead to an apprehension of deeper understanding, perhaps to a sublime moment. But there is a key division here between the natural and the fantastic sublime; Wordsworth may require nature to be something more than the actual in the sublime moment, but he also required actual nature, even if that nature would slip away, to become transparent so that one could see the world of the spirit, in the sublime moment. MacDonald pointed out that the ambiguity of Wordsworthian nature both as itself and as spiritual truth reflected the Christian paradox of God as immanent and transcendent, what Stephen Prickett calls "a fusion of Naturalistic and Platonic sentiments" (161). Nature in fantasy, of course, is never nature, only the image, and self-consciously so. How can one reconcile the authentic moment in nature of the Romantic sublime and the radically fictive fantastic sublime?

The natural sublime is anchored in the world of sense-experience; the fabulous is unmoored from reality. In the natural sublime, "the imagination is restricted to whatever is vivid and visible" in nature (Morris, *Religious Sublime*, 133); the fantastic makes new worlds. The figurative language of the fantastic engages the imagination by being self-consciously rhetorical; the natural sublime requires figuration to be transparent and affective (Montgomery, 329) in order for nature to dissolve and reveal the beyond.

This split informed Romanticism itself. How can the reader reconcile, for example, the strange fantastic figures in Coleridge's "Rime of the Ancient Mariner" of Death and Life-in-Death dicing for the souls of the crew, or the spirit nine fathoms deep, or the spell that holds the mariner in thrall in the poem from beginning to beyond the end, with the parable of natural piety beginning when the mariner shoots the albatross and ending when the mariner blesses the sea snakes unawares and the albatross falls from his neck? The two stories of "The Rime of the Ancient Mariner" are inextricably bound together, each moving the story along by turns. Neither can be removed without destroying the whole.

Wordsworth and Coleridge reconciled both fantastic and naturalistic poems as part of the one project of the *Lyrical Ballads* (1798). Coleridge describes their decision to write poems

> of two sorts. In one, the incidents and agents were to be, in part at least, supernatural; and the excellence aimed at was to consist in the interesting of the affections by the dramatic truth of such emotions as would naturally accompany such situations, supposing them real. And real in *this* sense they have been to every human being who, from whatever source of delusions, had at any time believed himself under supernatural agency. For the second class, subjects were to be chosen from ordinary life. (*Biographia*, 2:6)

As Wordsworth comments, however, even in the scenes drawn from ordinary life, they would "throw over them a certain coloring of the imagination" ("Preface," 791). The imagination, of course, or what Coleridge conjures up as the fantastic figure, "My shaping spirit of Imagination" ("Dejection," 86), binds the two sorts of poetry. Through the imagination both the fantastic and the natural can be the revelation of the sense sublime. Coleridge especially had been the poet of the fantastic imagination, yet Wordsworth had his moments, such as his wish for fantastic sights "that would make me less forlorn;/ Have sight of Proteus rising from he sea;/ Or hear old Triton blow his wreathed horn" ("The World is Too Much With Us," 12-4). Here Wordsworth too acknowledged the power of the fantastic to elevate the spirit. The weird and terrifying fantastic figures in Coleridge's "Mariner," "Kubla Khan" and "Christabel," the spirit nine fathoms deep, the pulsating sacred river, the beautiful/decrepit witch, can each be understood as representations of the Romantic overflow of feeling; they can be read, at least tentatively, as moments when the other world impinges, sometimes frighteningly, sometimes joyfully, but always irrationally and surprisingly, on the world of everyday experience.

In the end, the fantastic cannot be finally defined at all, of course; the fantastic image makes actual a negative presence, the frightening loss of self, the feeling of the movement of outside forces, of forces dimly understood or not understood. Discussing "Gothic Sublimity," David B. Morris writes that the Gothic sublime was inseparable from the antimimetic representations and exaggerations which implicitly announce their departure from a truth understood as probability or verisimilitude or representational form. If Freud is correct, the uncanny images of gothic sublimity--strangely familiar and yet defamiliarized--not only make contact with experience which lies outside of consciousness. They also maintain a new relation with language, whereby the descriptive and pictorial techniques of the eighteenth-century no longer carry the same function or value. What lies outside of consciousness also, as Lacan would tell us, lies outside of speech—or lies cryptically, fictively, irrevocably inscribed within a language that both is and is not our own. (311)

In the fantastic image, language provides something to stand in for the inexpressible. The fantastic encodes into language what cannot be said, says what cannot be known.

Thomas Weiskel comments that the sublime, as an image, "is the abyss" (25). Fantasy is also marked by an emptiness, filled only by language. In her essay "From Elfland to Poughkeepsie," the twentieth-century fantasist Ursula K. Le Guin asks why style, the use of a particularly, sometimes peculiarly, expressive language, is of such fundamental significance in fantastic literature, and answers:

because in fantasy there is nothing but the writer's vision of the world. There is no borrowed reality or history, or current events, or just plain folks at home in Peyton Place. There is no comfortable matrix of the common place to substitute for the imagination, to provide ready-made emotional response, and to disguise flaws and failures in creation. There is only a construct built in a void, with every joint and seam and nail exposed. To create what Tolkien calls "a secondary universe" is to make a new world. A world where no voice has ever spoken before; where the act of speech is the act of creation. The only voice that speaks is the creator's voice. And every word counts. (95)

MacDonald, in his essay "The Fantastic Imagination," comments, in a similar way: "To be able to live a moment in an imagined world, we must see the law of its existence obeyed" (314-5). As an example, MacDonald offered: "Suppose the gracious creatures of some child-like region of Fairyland talking either cockney or Gascon! Would not the tale, however lovely begun, sink at once to the level of the Burlesque—of all forms of literature the least worthy?" (315).

Le Guin agrees that the language of characters in fantasy fiction matters because it shows:

greatness of soul. . . . At least, it does in books. In life, we expect lapses. In naturalistic fiction, too, we expect lapses, and laugh at an 'overheroic' hero. But in fantasy, which, instead of imitating the perceived confusion and complexity of existence, tries to hint at an order and clarity underlying existence--in fantasy, we need not compromise. Every word spoken is meaningful. (87-8)

In fantasy, the creation stands alone, provoking a response only through a kind of daring performance of words, a high-wire act over an emptiness, suggesting something above nothing or a light in the abyss.

The natural sublime offered nature and turned out to be lying. The fantastic lies and so hints at truth, leaving the reader groping after the actual of which the lie is the obvious difference. The fundamental characteristic of fantasy is displacement. However, fantasy's displacement from the real is and can only be defined in relation to the real, or rather, to our notion of reality, a notion changeable from time, place and person. As the critic Sandor remarks:

Fantastic stories are not true to the actual world but what is known of the actual world is both limited and questionable. (350)

In his essay "Wishful Thinking—or Hopeful Dreaming?" the twentieth-century fantasist Lloyd Alexander describes naturalistic literature and fantasy literature as inextricably bound together, each in the end simply a kind of interpretation and presentation of the real:

All art, by definition of the word, is fantasy in the broadest sense. The most uncompromisingly (should I say sordidly?) naturalistic novel is still a manipulation of reality. Fantasy, too, is a manipulation of reality. There is no essential conflict or contradiction between literary realism and literary fantasy, any more than between science and humanism. Technical details aside, most of the things you can say about fantasy also apply to realism. I suppose you might define realism as fantasy pretending to be true; and fantasy as reality pretending to be a dream. (143)

From a certain point of view, the difference between fantastic literature and naturalistic literature is a matter of honesty; fantasy knows itself to be fantasy, the imagination unbound. In his book *The Romantic Fantastic*, the critic Tobin Siebers writes of fantastic literature, and especially what he calls "the Romantic fantastic," that it, "by virtue of its themes and structures, reveals more boldly than other literary forms the role of superstition in all artistic representation" (20). Siebers defines superstition as "what critical discourse calls 'magical thought'" (12), the unconscious logic of dream causality.

Fantasy has undeniable connections to dreams and to madness, that is, to the unconscious. But that must not obscure fantasy's position as art, as the imagination not simply at play, not only producing "escapist" literature, but as the imagination at work. Tolkien answered the "escapism" charge against fantasy by insisting on the right of the individual to seek beyond the confines of the world, that is, for the unlawfully held prisoner to try to get out and go home. He accused those who made the charge of escapism against fantastic literature of confusing escape with desertion (148). Sandor comments:

People who castigate fantastic stories for being escapist can only do it in the name of some authority which is considered obvious, unproblematic, and in no need of legitimation. (350)

Fantasy never ultimately departs reality. In a complex relationship with reality, fantasy comments on it, stretches it, and interprets it. In attempts at definition, one can only rely on collective truth and say of the fantastic, "I know it when I see it." But one never really does. Ultimately, a certain elusiveness is its only mark.

In his work *The Romantic Fantastic*, the critic Tobin Siebers points out that the link between the Romantic and the fantastic lies in their shared movement towards something other, towards the irrational or supernatural, towards what Siebers calls "difference":

It is not surprising that the fantastic emerged during the Romantic period, for it is perhaps the supreme literature of difference. Romanticism was a movement of poetic lyricism, artistic rebellion, and personal idiosyncrasy. The Romantic writers of the nineteenth century wanted to create original works of art, but they also strove to achieve a degree of personal difference. Fantastic literature enshrines differences, highlighting those aspects of experience that venture beyond the strictly human toward a supernatural realm. In fantastic literature, the visionary poetics of the Romantic individual and the superstitious nightmares of the common men converge, affirming idiosyncrasy, originality, and difference on all fronts. (9)

Fantasy's self-conscious displacement evokes the repressed from one's self-creation of reality. Fantasy's otherness, in turn, presses one to ask, "What is it?" It is not only open to interpretation, but positively requires it. As MacDonald insists of his literary fairy tales:

It cannot help having some meaning; if it has proportion and harmony it has vitality, and vitality is truth. The beauty may be plainer than the truth, but without the truth the beauty could not be, and the fairy tale would give no delight. ("Fantastic Imagination," 316)

For MacDonald, the vitality of fantastic images themselves, something living within them, cannot help but have meaning.

In a similar vein, Le Guin comments on fantasy

as art, not spontaneous play, its affinity is not with daydream, but with dream. It is a different approach to reality, an alternative technique for apprehending and coping with existence. It is not anti-rational, but para-rational; not realistic, but surrealistic, superrealistic, a heightening of reality. (84)

Le Guin connects fantastic literature and psychoanalysis, noting that fantastic literature is akin to Freud's "primary, not secondary process thinking," and that "It employs archetypes, which, as Jung warned us, are dangerous things" (84). Le Guin writes:

Fantasy is nearer to poetry, to mysticism, and to insanity than naturalistic fiction is. It is a real wilderness, and those who go there shouldn't feel too safe. (84)

Le Guin comments that fantasy literature "is a journey into the subconscious mind, just as psychoanalysis is. Like psychoanalysis, it can be dangerous; and *it will change you*" (93). In fantasy literature, the reader is invited, perhaps tricked by Will o' Wisps, into the primeval forest. As the simple power of the fairy tale narrative proves, no seeker comes into the forests of Faerie without wanting, without needing to come there. And nobody returns unchanged.

Chapter 7

The Fantastic Sublime in Kenneth Grahame's *The Wind in the Willows*

The chapter-by-chapter alternation between the parallel adventures of Mole and of Toad in *The Wind in the Willows* establishes Toad as an exaggerated, comic counterpoint to Mole. Mole's Romantic endeavors may be told affectionately and playfully, but the visionary in his story is always reverenced; Toad's mock-Romantic strivings, mad driving and car wrecks, are always ludicrous. Michael Mendelson, in an article on the plotting of *The Wind in the Willows*, first outlined the critic Peter Green's argument that the Toad incidents were probably composed first, Mole's only later (Green, ch. 11), and then comments on the parallel "calls to adventure" and their outcomes:

In chapter 1, when Mole grabs the oars of the scull, Rat cries, "Stop it you silly ass . . . . You'll have us over," and the damp, repentant Mole quickly acknowledges, "Indeed I have been a complete ass, and I know it." By contrast, when the Toad sits overturned in the road, "spellbound," it is the Mole who says, "O, stop being an ass, Toad." The "crazed" Toad can only dream of renewed risks "on my reckless way." By changing the initial order of composition and placing Mole's springtime adventure of emancipation first, Grahame establishes a dominant mood of temperate indulgence alongside of which the overheated, midsummer's extravagance of the Toad, while charming, seems nonetheless an aberrant response to the call. (130)

Toad is foolish and learns nothing. Having been overturned in a caravan, he buys a car and overturns that, then buys more cars. He wants more, faster while Mole stays true to the steadier, slower pastime of messing about in boats.

Grahame is "demonstrating in Toad the problems of an unexamined life devoted to acquisition and external adventure in a world that is retreating further and further from nature" (Poss, 86). But the split between Mole and Toad does not mark a clean break between Nature (good) and Technology (bad). Pan, a manifestation of the sacred in Nature, lives on The River. But The River cannot be simply identified as Nature. The Wild Wood where Mole loses himself to the Terror of the Wild Wood is nature as well. But it is a dangerous place of wild excess compared with the gentler life on the riverbank. In *The Wind in the Willows*, the sacred is not found in the deeper wilds, but rather on small river islands, or in picnicking on lazy-day boating trips.

Rat and Mole picnic and loaf, which in Grahame's works is a kind of prayer, not in innocent and untrammeled wilderness, but in a place of compromise between Nature and Comfort along the domesticated riverbank. *The Wind in the Willows* is ultimately the champion not of Nature, but of the Rural, the cultivated countryside of distant but friendly neighbors and dusty roads. Instead of being antitechnological, a certain level of technology is positively required, enough to build manor houses and roads from the primeval forest, and boats and carts in which to get around. Driving, in *The Wind in the Willows*, can be characterized as a shallow, disconcerting, disconnected part of the Wide World which Rat abhors:

"Beyond the Wild Wood comes the Wide World," said the Rat. "And that's something that doesn't matter, either to you or me. I've never been there, and I'm never going, nor you, either, if you've got any sense at all. Don't ever return to it again if you please. Now then! Here's our backwater at last, where we're going to lunch." (ch. 1; 11-2)

Yet, Technology is not simply demonized, but is rather deplored as an end in itself.

For Toad, motor cars *are* an end in themselves, a poor choice in his unseemly pursuit of the ecstatic. While Mole errs on the side of the Wild Wood, wandering in too deep, Toad errs on the other side, toward the fleeting and insubstantial, toward driving. "Poop, poop!" (ch. 2; 38) Toad says in a comic exclamation of glassy-eyed joy when he first sees a motorcar.

"The *real* way to travel! The *only* way to travel! Here to-day—in next week to-morrow! Villages skipped, towns and cities jumped—always somebody else's horizon! O bliss! O poop-poop! O my! O my!" (ch. 2; 38)

Toad acquires his cars on impulse. In an excess of driving lust, Toad even steals a car although he has plenty of money. Toad crashed at least eight cars, the final two someone else's. Toad's coach house is, according to Rat, "literally piled up to the roof . . . with fragments of motor-cars none of them bigger than your hat" (ch. 4; 68). For stealing a car, he winds up in a dungeon, a dejected toad.

Toad's lack of foresight and poor driving skills are clear enough even before he owns any cars. In our first encounter with Toad, he rows his boat too fast and overturns it. Driving motor cars magnifies the tragic, or rather, comic flaws of Toad. Toad never drives a car but he drives it fast, as fast as he can go until he crashes. His arrogance is inflated, and sometimes even sinister, rising to a manic pitch:

as if in a dream, all sense of right and wrong, all fear of obvious consequences, seemed temporarily suspended. He increased his pace, and as the car devoured the street and leapt forth on the high road though the open country, he was only conscious that he was Toad once more, Toad at his best and highest, Toad the terror, the traffic-queller, the Lord of the lone trail, before whom all must give way or be smitten into nothingness and everlasting night. He chanted as he flew, and the car responded with sonorous drone; the miles were eaten up under him as he sped he knew not whither, fulfilling his instincts, living his hour, reckless of what might come to him. (ch. 6; 121)

In this moment, Toad appears a touch Byronic in his Romantic seeking. Coleridge, in the "Statesmen's Manual," warns against the danger of the Satanic Romantic hero, modeled on Milton's Satan and exemplified by the protagonists in Byron's romances. For Coleridge, the individual Will is an expression of wisdom and love coming from God and returning to Him, but "in its utmost abstraction and consequent state of reprobation, the Will becomes the satanic pride and rebellious self-idolatry in the relations of the spirit to itself, and remorseless despotism relatively to others" (65). Toad is certainly no Satan—he is far too much fun—but there is something of the dark hero in him. His pride does wax to awful hubris: boastful songs, petty pouts and spiteful or self-aggrandizing comments.

According to the critic David Gooderson, in his preface to Grahame's letters to his son Alastair, which outline much of Toad's adventures, the stories were written "with gently satirical intent" because of Alastair's "tendency to exult in his exploits" (11). Toad never succeeds but he must exult with arrogant self-congratulation, as when he escaped from Rat's care:

tying one end of the improvised rope round the central mullion of the handsome Tudor window which formed such a feature of his bedroom, he scrambled out, slid lightly to the ground, and, taking the opposite direction to the Rat, marched off lightheartededly, whistling a merry tune. (ch. 6; 117)

Gooderson comments: "Isn't it the whistling a merry tune that instills some ill-will towards Toad? We love him and wish and wait for another mis-deed, yet the over-reaching quality, the heedlessness of friends, is deplorable" (11). Grahame clearly, as Gooderson points out, loves Toad as well, and exults in his excesses even as he condemns them, especially Toad's imaginative, wild talk. As Toad admits in a characteristic moment of bombast:

perhaps I am a bit of a talker. A popular fellow such as I am—my friends get round me—we chaff, we sparkle, we tell witty stories—and somehow my tongue gets to wagging. I have the gift of conversation. I've been told I ought to have a *salon*, whatever that may be. (ch. 11; 231)

The narrator of *The Wind in the Willows* writes of Toad's hearty and excessive talk:

Much that he related belonged more properly to the category of what-might have happened-had-I-only-thought-of-it-in-time-instead-of-ten-minutes-afterwards. Those are always the best and raciest adventures; and why should they not be truly ours, as much as the somewhat inadequate things that really come off?" (ch. 11; 238)

Toad is exactly what is most fun, if wickedly fun, about selfish desire; he is the petty satisfaction of the witty comeback or, in startling contrast to the innocence of the Wordsworthian child, of childishness and covetousness.

Mole, in contrast, is like a Wordsworthian child who has turned himself outward in innocence to nature. Like the true Coleridgean Romantic, there he may find himself moved toward an unconscious affirmation of the strange beauty of creation: "I blessed them unaware" (286), says the Ancient Mariner when all seems hopeless and dead, and the universe comes alive.

In his Romantic longings, Mole is apprenticed to Rat who was a poet—he "scribbled poetry" (ch. 3; 44) and "tried over rhymes that wouldn't fit" (46)—and had lived a long time beside The River following the sacred pastime of "messing about in boats." Rat not only saves Mole from drowning after Mole grabbed the oars and tipped over the boat early in the novel, but, much later and much more bravely, rises from his "half-finished verses" (51) to save Mole from another dangerous encounter with nature in the Terror of the Wild Wood.

Rat's poetic ear also first hears, clearly, the "song-dream" of Pan in the willows, which leads to a "holy place" (ch. 7; 134), Pan's sacred island. Rat says of the piping of Pan:

So beautiful and strange and new! Since it was to end so soon I wish I had never heard it. For it has roused a longing in me that is pain, and nothing seems worth while but just to hear that sound once more and go on listening to it for ever. (132)

When Rat and Mole follow Pan's piping into the heart of nature, they see, to quote Wordsworth, "into the life of things" ("Tintern Abbey," 49). Nature becomes at every moment more vivid: "The horizon became clearer, field and tree came more into sight, and somehow with a different look; the mystery began to drop away" (ch. 7; 132). Wordsworth describes the experience of nature in a visionary state as "the glory and the freshness of a dream" ("Ode," 5). For Mole and Rat, the rich meadow-grass seemed that morning of freshness and a greenness unsurpassable. Never had they noticed the roses so vivid, the willow-herb so riotous, the meadow-sweet so odorous and pervading. (133)

Coleridge describes something similar when he writes of how:

> my friend
> Struck with deep joy may stand, as I have stood,
> Silent with swimming sense; yea, gazing round
> On the wide landscape, gaze till all doth seem
> Less gross than bodily; and of such hues
> As veil the Almighty spirit, when he yet makes
> Spirits perceive his presence. ("Lime Tree Bower," 37-43)

The world of the riverbank, under the spell of Pan's pipes, that is, the wind in the willows, is exposed as but a gloss over the world of the spirit. When Mole and Rat open their eyes in a visionary way, the world opens up—through intense and surprising colors, the perception of a mystic music that reveals an inner harmony, and the calling up of deep feeling—and reveals its sacred heart. In *The Wind in the Willows*, the rending of the veil between worlds leads to the same perception as in Coleridge's poem of a presence—an "Almighty spirit"—in nature:

Mole felt a great Awe. . . . no panic terror—indeed he felt wonderfully at peace and happy—but it was an awe that smote and held him and, without seeing, he knew it could only mean that some august Presence was very, very near. (135)

Wordsworth also describes the natural sublime in just such terms—an actual presence, an awe and a fear: "I have felt/ A presence that disturbs me with the joy/ Of elevated thoughts; a sense sublime" ("Tintern," 93-5), and in *The Prelude* such an apprehension of a presence is "Fostered alike by beauty and by fear" (Bk. 1: line 302). Wordsworth's fear is the fear of blockage, of the loss of identity without transcendence; the joy is the transcendent moment of the sublime revealed.

Similarly, when Pan appears to Rat and Mole, they worship him with a joy that is also fear.

"Afraid?" murmured Rat, his eyes shining with unutterable love. "Afraid! Of *Him?* O, never, never! And yet—and yet—O, Mole, I am afraid!"

Then the two animals crouching to the earth, bowed their heads and did worship. (136)

Rat's love is unutterable, beyond language or understanding, "too deep for tears" ("Ode," 203), in a typical Romantic movement beyond the describable. The exclamation "O," common in Romantic poetry, marks into language the indescribable overflow of feeling when time and place loosen their hold on the individual in epiphanies of imaginative experience—epiphanies beyond the language that binds one into an understanding of the world and the self.

In the fantastic sublime, Pan appears in actual form, while the glory in nature for Wordsworth is always "marked as much by absence as by presence, the sublime of negation" (Gillin, 173). Too much can be made of this, however, as too much can be made of the Romantics' inability in the end to define the sublime; the fantastic is also a negative presence, a presence without actual presence—the fantastic figure standing for something unknowable and undefinable. At some level one must take Wordsworth at face value, that is, must take his indication of a negative presence, his inability to speak, as the actual presence of something unspeakable, not simply a failure of words, but a success of the sublime.

Either way, negative or actual presence, the fantastic figure in Grahame's work lives out the Romantic sublime perfectly. Pan, god in nature,

the kindly demigod is careful to bestow on those to whom he has revealed himself in their helping: the gift of forgetfulness. Lest the awful remembrance should remain and grow, and overshadow mirth and pleasure, and the great haunting memory should spoil all the after-lives of little animals helped out of difficulties, in order that they should be happy and light-hearted as before. (136)

Weiskel's third, or reactive phase, of the sublime restores the balance between inner and outer, or outer and beyond. This restorative phase is marked by a sublime forgetfulness as the self is reconstructed. Yet the fall back into language, into place, time, person, also produces a desolate feeling of separation as the recovery of the self requires the loss of the universal but leaves behind a requisite trace memory. Wordsworth's memory of glory—despite sublime forgetfulness—haunts him: "there has passed away a glory from the earth" ("Ode," 18). A momentary vision of sacred nature can, as Pan feared, bring regret of holiness lost: "The pansy at my feet/ Doth the same tale repeat; Whither is fled the visionary gleam?/ Where is it now, the glory and the dream?" (54-7).

Rat, a poet with a poet's ear, senses similar intimations of a glory passed away. Even after the forgetfulness of Pan, as Mole and Rat are floating home downstream, Mole remarks how tired he feels, "and yet nothing particular has happened" (140). Rat replies: "Or Something very surprising and splendid and beautiful." He calls to Mole: "hark to the wind playing in the reeds!" He yet hears the eternal.

> "It's like music—far away music," said the Mole, nodding drowsily.
> "So I was thinking," murmured the Rat, dreamful and languid.
> "Dance music—the lilting sort that runs on without a stop—but with words in it, too—it passes into words and out of them again—I catch them at intervals—then it is dance music once more, and then nothing but the reeds' soft thin whispering"
> "You hear better than I," said the Mole sadly. "I cannot catch the words." (140)

The wind in the willows is like Wordsworth's visionary "light" ("Ode," 69), or, in keeping with the image of the willows, "splendor in the grass" (178), which did "fade into the light of common day" (76), but not without leaving behind a haunting memory of the sublime moment.

The wind through the reeds moves Rat to longing as the Romantic wind upon the Æolian harp causes the welling of feeling in the poet. Coleridge writes of the Æolian harp:

> And what if all of animated nature,
> Be but organic Harps diversely framed,
> That tremble into thought, as o'er them sweeps
> Plastic and vast, one intellectual breeze,
> At once the soul of each, and God of all? ("Eolian Harp," 44-8)

Coleridge in this poem enlarges the image of the "correspondent breeze" upon the wind-harp by making all of nature the harp upon which the motion of an inner spirit expresses itself. The wind in the willows is Grahame's image for exactly that—the presence of spirit moving through everything in nature, an invisible motion felt and a distant music heard, always nearby but always out of reach.

All in a Romantic spontaneous moment, as Rat and Mole row homeward, Rat hears and recites a poem of Pan heard in the wind in the reeds, but "It is hard to catch and grows each minute fainter" (141). Rat cries out:

"Ah! now they return again, and this time full and clear! This time, at last, it is the real, the unmistakable thing, simple—passionate—perfect—" (141)

Rat falls asleep without another word. "The Winds come to me from the fields of sleep" ("Ode," 28), as Wordsworth writes enigmatically, which might mean: they come from outside the waking world, outside consciousness. The sublime always lies just beyond perception, as the unconscious to the conscious.

The Wind in the Willows presents the dangers as well as the glory of the fantastic sublime, the moment of blockage or fragmentation implicit in Coleridge's formulation of the Romantic imagination, which "dissolves, diffuses, dissipates in order to recreate" (*Biographia*, 1:304). In one slight but memorable comic scene of blockage, picnic food is described to excess as Rat enumerates the contents of a picnic basket:

"There's cold chicken inside it," replied the Rat briefly; "coldtonguecoldhamcoldbeefpickledgherkinssaladfrenchrollscressandwidgespotted meatgingerbeerlemonadesodawater—"

"O stop, stop," cried the Mole in ecstasies: "This is too much!" (ch. 1; 8)

Another scene, however, Mole's long night of the soul in the Wild Wood, expresses the blockage and fragmentation of the fantastic sublime without any comic undertones.

The critic Peter Hunt describes how "the Mole, in a moment of pride or, more classically, hubris, 'slips out' to go to the Wild Wood alone, and approaches his nadir, the low point of his existence.

Everything in the Wild Wood is the opposite of the riverbank house—cold, dark, threatening and uncertain" (*Wind*, 36). Mole's emotional experience of the Wild Wood is also the opposite of his ecstatic reaction on first encountering The River; terror replaces joy, as the failure of the sublime replaces the successful sublime moment. Wordsworth writes, concerning those twin aspects of the sublime, beauty and fear, that "Presences" in nature "Impressed upon all forms the characters/ Of danger or desire; and thus did make/ The surface of the universal earth/ With triumph and delight, with hope and fear,/ Work like a sea" (*Prelude*, 1: 464-74). The sea of faces Mole sees in his experience of the Terror of the Wild Wood is just such an endless repetition of the fear, not the hope, but the terrifying infinity of the sublime, the overwhelming feeling coming without the compensatory release, only fragmentation, both endless and broken.

In chapter 3, "The Wild Wood," Mole travels out alone, against Rat's advice, into the Wild Wood. It becomes dark. He turns off the path and quickly becomes lost. He feels himself watched:

> He passed another hole, and another, and another; and then—yes!—no!—yes! certainly a little narrow face, with hard eyes, had flashed up for an instant from a hole, and was gone. He hesitated—braced himself up for an effort and strode on. Then suddenly, as if it had been so all the time, every hole, far and near, and there were hundreds of them, seemed to possess its face, coming and going rapidly, all fixing on him glances of malice and hatred: all hard-eyed and evil and sharp.
>
> If he could only get away from the holes in the banks, he thought, there would be no more faces. He swung off the path and plunged into the untrodden places of the wood.
>
> Then the whistling began.
>
> Very faint and shrill it was, and far behind him, when first he heard it; but somehow it made him hurry forward. Then, still very faint and shrill, it sounded far ahead of him, and made him hesitate and want to go back. As he halted in indecision it broke out on either side, and seemed to be caught up and passed on throughout the whole length of the wood to its farthest limit. They were up and alert and ready, evidently, whoever they were! And he—he was alone, and unarmed, and far from any help; and the night was closing in.
>
> Then the pattering began.
>
> He thought it was only falling leaves at first, so slight and delicate was the sound of it. Then as it grew it took a regular rhythm, and he knew it for nothing else but the pit-pat of little feet, still a very long way off. Was it in

front or behind? It seemed to be first one, then the other, then both. It grew and multiplied, till from every quarter as he listened anxiously, leaning this way and that, it seemed to be closing in on him. . . .

The pattering increased till it sounded like a sudden hail on the dry-leaf carpet spread around him. The whole wood seemed running now, running hard, hunting, chasing, closing in round something or—somebody? In panic, he began to run too, aimlessly, he knew not whither. He ran up against things, he fell over things and into things, he darted under things and dodged around things. . . . [H]e knew it at last, in all its fullness, that dread thing which other little dwellers in field and hedgerow had encountered here, and known as their darkest moment—that thing which the Rat had vainly tried to shield him from —the Terror of the Wild Wood! (48-50)

Distance and direction fall away, mocking him; sounds seem both innocent and menacing, both falling leaves and pattering feet; he is indecisive and suffocating, panicked and lost; yet nothing, absolutely nothing is palpable, no enemy can be clearly discovered except an inner enemy, except fear, naked and absolute. He is fragmented and in despair, lost in the failed sublime where all the world is one except for the overwhelmed and insignificant self, all is in conspiracy against the self. Mole is saved only by the courage and presence of mind of his friend Rat who comes into the Wild Wood, well armed, to get him, and also by their discovery, deep in the snowy wood, of Badger's safe burrow.

Mole had been unwary and foolish in venturing into the Wild Wood alone after Rat had warned him, as he had been foolish when he overturned the boat and Toad had been an ass with his car crack-ups, but the dangers of the sublime are not only for the foolish. The most sensitive heart is also at peril. Coleridge writes of the overwhelming power of the ecstatic poet:

> Beware! Beware!
> His flashing eyes, his floating hair!
> Weave a circle around him thrice,
> and close your eyes with holy dread,
> For he on honeydew hath fed,
> And drunk the milk of paradise. ("Kubla Khan," 49-54)

Rat speaks "as if in a trance" (136) even on the way to Pan's island; he is "Entranced . . . spellbound" (132), and "the intoxicating melody imposed its will on Mole, and mechanically he bent to the oars again" (133). All too easily the sublime may reduce one to an automaton, moving at the whim and will of strange influences. The aimless Romantic searcher may be taken up by outside forces to terrible consequence, as Christabel is by the dread power she finds, or that finds her, while she is in (apparently) innocent prayer in the woods, or as Wordsworth is when he suddenly became aware of "a huge peak, black and huge" looming above the lake during the boat-stealing incident in *The Prelude*. It

> Towered up between me and the stars, and still,
> For so it seemed, with purpose of its own,
> And measured motion, like a living Thing
> Strode after me. (1: 382-5)

In *The Wind in the Willows*, Rat also discovers the dangers of the Romantic seeker in chapter 9, "Wayfarers All." Wandering aimlessly, filled with a sense of longing as the other animals prepare to migrate and follow "the call of the South, of the South" (170), Rat meets up with the wayfarer heading toward the sea. Some of the description of the wayfarer, "lean and keen-featured, and somewhat bowed at the shoulders; his paws were thin and long, his eyes much wrinkled at the corners" (173), may remind one of the Ancient Mariner "with his skinny hand," "the ancient man" (9, 19), perhaps bowed by the weight he had carried around his neck. As the Ancient Mariner must "pass, like night, from land to land" (586) and tell his tale, so the Sea Rat spins a yarn of travel and adventure, holding the Water Rat "silent and enthralled, [as he] floated on dream canals and heard a phantom song pealing high between vaporous grey wave-lapped walls" (177), a phantom song perhaps something like "A woman wailing for her demon lover!" (16) in Coleridge's "Kubla Khan." The Sea Rat tells of journeys in the South, as the Mariner journeyed to the South Pole; from both, the word "South" may strike one as subterranean and secret.

The Seafarer held Rat "Spellbound and quivering with excitement" (181); in the same way, the Wedding Guest is spellbound. The Mariner "holds him [the Wedding Guest] with his glittering eye" (3) as the Seafarer, his eye lit with a brightness that seemed caught from some far-away sea-beacon, filled his glass with the vintage of the South, and, leaning towards the Water Rat, compelled his gaze and held him, body and soul, while he talked. Those eyes were of the changing foam-streaked grey-green of leaping Northern Seas. (182)

As the Wedding-Guest "cannot choose but hear" (38), enspelled by the Mariner's voice, so the Water Rat is held by

the talk, the wonderful talk flowed on—or was it speech entirely, or did it pass at times into song—chanty of the sailors weighing the dripping anchor, sonorous hum of the shrouds in a tearing North-Easter, ballad of the fisherman hauling his nets at sundown against an apricot sky, chords of guitar and mandoline from gondola or caique? Did it change into the cry of the wind, plaintive at first, angrily shrill as it freshened, rising to a tearing whistle, sinking to a musical trickle of air from the leech of the bellying sail? All these sounds the spellbound listener seemed to hear, and with them the hungry complaint of the gulls and the sea-mews, the soft thunder of the breaking wave. . . . (183)

At the end of the tale, the spellbound Rat is "like a sleep-walker; listening ever with parted lips" (185), as the Wedding Guest at the end of the Mariner's tale is "stunned,/ And is of sense forlorn" (622-3). Rat packs up to follow the call of the South and his friend Mole must forcibly convince him to stay. Mole hides his pack and "turned his talk to the harvest . . . and the large moon rising over the acres dotted with sheaves" (187-8), to home and hearth and harvest. He brings Rat "a pencil and a few half-sheets of paper" (188), reminding him how it has been a long time since he had written any poetry. The Wedding Guest cannot return to his wedding, the simple grace of society. Haunted by the tale of the Mariner, "A sadder and a wiser man,/ He rose the morrow morn" (624-5). For Rat, although he was certainly a wiser and a sadder Rat, in writing poetry instead of brooding, "the cure had at least begun" (188).

Home balances Romantic vision in *The Wind in the Willows*. It is respite and renewal. In chapter 5, "Dulce Domum," Mole (with the help of Rat) rediscovers the need of the wise visionary for the refuge and focus of a home. Returning to his long-abandoned, still unwhitewashed house after a long stay with Rat by the river, he discovered how much it all meant to him, and the special value of some anchorage in one's existence. He did not want at all to abandon the new life and its splendid spaces, to turn his back on the sun and air and all they offered him and creep home and stay there; the upper world was all too strong, it called to him still. . . But it was good to think he had this to come back to, this place which was all his own, these things which were so glad to see him again and could always be counted upon. . . . (103)

The return home is a common motif in fantastic literature, perhaps a necessary balance to the estrangement of the fantastic, the disconcerting presence of what Tolkien calls Faerie, the other world. Tolkien's *The Hobbit* is sub-titled "There and Back Again," and the last line of his *Lord of the Rings* is Sam's greeting to his wife: "Well, I'm back." Mole's homecoming is enacted easily enough, as is Rat's, a tribute to their more dignified pursuit of the ecstatic. For Toad, there is a "Scouring of the Shire" to face. As a direct result of his misadventures in motor cars, he is required to fight for his lost home.

For the sin of driving, Toad loses control of his home, a representation of his own personal loss of control. Toad is a comic Odysseus (as the title of the last chapter, "The Return of Ulysses," emphasizes), home from his Great Wanderings to find his stately home, commonly called the "best house in these parts" (4), taken over by invaders. Penelope's suitors are played by the stoats and weasels who jumped on the opportunity of Toad's incarceration for car stealing to overrun his home in great numbers, set up guards against Toad's friends and eat up his larder in big and unruly celebrations. Badger, Rat and Mole join Toad in a mock-epic battle to rout the stoats and weasels and regain Toad Hall in a definitive victory for home and friendship.

Mole and Toad are apprenticed as Romantic seekers to two teachers, Rat and Badger. Rat stands as the Romantic poet and wise visionary; Badger, the only one of the four who is never in danger of losing or abandoning his home, is the solid, simple patriarch of the safe house in the midst of the Wild Wood. As Lois R. Kuznets observed, "Badger lives deepest down," he is the most deeply rooted, and Mole lives at an intermediate distance between Rat on the riverbank and Badger deep underground (119). The sublime is associated with the out-of-doors and the open air; Badger knows nothing of these pleasures, but treasures the great, secret tunnels of his home:

"There's no security, or peace and tranquility, except underground. . . . No builders, no tradesman, no remarks passed on you by fellows looking over your wall, and, above all, no *weather.* . . . No, up and out of doors is good enough to roam around and get one's living in; but underground to come back to at last—that's my idea of *home!"* (76; ch. 4)

Toad, who lives farthest above ground in an overly grandiose house, has no balance. He drives his fast cars and crashes, losing home and everything; Badger often insults him gruffly, relenting only after Toad Hall is regained. Mole, on the other hand, is balanced safely between Rat and Badger. Both Rat and Badger initiate Mole into their secrets: Rat taking Mole with him to Pan's island at the heart of the river; Badger showing Mole his amazing and extensive underground home, and praising him during the battle for Toad's dwelling. The clever apprentice of these two wise teachers, Mole, in "Wayfarers All," reteaches Rat what he already knew (and had helped remind Mole in "Dulce Domum"): the necessary balance of Romantic longing and transcendence with the contentment and love of home.

The Wind in the Willows ends happily with banquets, friends and lavish eating. Toad, one is assured, "was indeed an altered Toad!" (ch. 12; 257), although one doubts it. Mole, however, has truly found a better life as a Romantic seeker of the sublime, but a seeker with some anchorage in his existence—the love of home and the love of friends.

Chapter 8

The Fantastic Sublime in George MacDonald's *At the Back of the North Wind*

As Kenneth Grahame's *The Wind in the Willows* followed the parallel adventures of Toad and Mole, George MacDonald's *At the Back of the North Wind* alternates between the parallel adventures of Diamond in a realistic, poverty stricken Victorian London and in a dream world with his spirit-guide North Wind who leads him to the land back of the north wind. No strict demarcation separates Diamond's dream and waking worlds. Although North Wind often comes at night just as Diamond falls asleep, once she comes in the day, and once she sets Diamond down in a real London street when he demands to help a poor street sweeper named Nanny.

In his realistic adventures, he is the son of a cab driver and sleeps in a hayloft over the stable where his father's reliable coach horse, Old Diamond, lives. Young Diamond is preternaturally good. He befriends the little street sweeper, Nanny, giving her aid and comfort. He looks after his new baby sister, singing her pleasing nonsense songs. When his family is in financial distress and his father ill, he takes Old Diamond out and works as a cab driver, helped out by the other cabbies because he is their "favorite" due to his seemingly impossible kindness. He is considered a sweet idiot, blessed by heaven; as Nanny said, tapping her forehead: "'The cabbies call him God's baby,' she whispered. 'He's not right in the head you know. A tile loose'" (ch. 19; 163). Diamond only smiles at the name, taking it as a compliment. In a testament to the redemptive power of his goodness, he even helps a cabbie, a drunken father and abusive husband, take steps toward a new and better way of life.

In his dream world adventures, Diamond moves more easily into the world of the spirit than Rat and Mole, or for that matter, Wordsworth and Coleridge. Only twice does he experience the fantastic sublime as fear, that is, in its twin aspects as a beauty, or awe, that is also terror. First, as quoted at the beginning of chapter 5, Diamond hides under his bedclothes at North Wind's initial appearance in his hayloft bedroom; in that instance, North Wind summarily blows the covers off him. Second, while flying tangled up in North Wind's infinite hair, Diamond suddenly sees a cathedral loom up to blot out the stars.

"Look then," said North Wind; and with one sweep of her great white arm, she swept yards deep of darkness [her hair] like a great curtain from before the face of the boy.

And lo! it was a blue night, lit up with stars. Where it did not shine with stars it shimmered with the milk of the stars, except where, just opposite to Diamond's face the grey towers of a cathedral blotted out each its own shape of sky and stars.

"Oh! what's that?" cried Diamond, struck with a kind of terror, for he had never seen a cathedral, and it rose before him with an awful reality in the midst of the wide spaces, conquering emptiness with grandeur." (ch. 7; 67)

The cathedral towers rise up to blot out the sky, just as the towering peak "Upreared its head. . . . between me and the stars" (I: 380-2) in the boat-stealing incident from *The Prelude*. Wordsworth shrank away in fear from the looming peak, which seemed to stride after him.

> With trembling oars I turned,
> And through the silent water stole my way
> Back to the covert of the willow tree. (I: 385-7)

The disturbing incident left behind "huge and mighty forms," images that Wordsworth found "were a trouble to my dreams" (I: 398-400).

In MacDonald's work, North Wind does not allow Diamond to turn away. Both times Diamond shows fear, North Wind demands that he put his faith in her absolutely. At his fear at their first meeting, she tells Diamond: "Just you believe what I say, and do as I tell you" (ch. 1; 12). When Diamond does not do as she says, she forces the issue, blowing the bedcovers off him, presenting herself before him, entrancing him with her beauty, mastering his fear. She apologizes only later that she "was forced to be so rough with you" (15). Rat and Mole, like Wordsworth and Coleridge, found fear to be a natural part of the sublime experience, but North Wind will not tolerate it from Diamond.

When Diamond asks about the cathedral, North Wind straightaway takes him into it and onto a narrow ledge around the central part of the church where Diamond's fear is heightened:

Diamond saw nothing to keep him from falling into the church. It lay below him like a great silent gulf hollowed in stone, and he held his breath for fear as he looked down. (ch. 7; 68)

Diamond experiences the natural fear of sublime failure, the failure of the abyss, the "great silent gulf" that might swallow self and all. When Diamond admits his fear to North Wind, however, she is unsympathetic, and once again forced to be rough.

"But I have hold of you, I tell you, foolish child,"
"Yes, but somehow I can't feel comfortable."
"If you were to fall, and my hold of you were to give way, I should be down after you in less moment than a lady's watch can tick, and catch you long before you reach the ground."
"I don't like it, though," said Diamond.
"*Oh! oh! oh!*" he screamed the next moment, bent double with terror, for North Wind had let go her hold of his hand, and vanished. . . .
She left the words "Come after me," sounding in his ears. (68-9)

When Diamond takes courage and walks along the ledge, he finds North Wind waiting for him. She explains: "I couldn't hold a little coward to my heart. It would make me so cold!" Diamond must have faith as only a Wordsworthian child, still more of heaven than of earth, can have faith. He gives himself fully to the world of the spirit in a way Rat and Mole cannot. Rat and Mole, after all, are adults, animal-adults, but nonetheless independent and home owners. They are divided between their Romantic longings and the very real pleasures and comfort of this world—food, especially, and home, that "anchorage in one's existence." Rat and Mole receive no more than a glimpse of the "august Presence" embodied by Pan. Diamond's adventures with North Wind only begin with such a face-to-face meeting with a divine presence. Thus, his adventures in pursuit of the sublime moment essentially start where Rat and Mole's *end*.

Diamond's adventures do not lead him toward a balance between sublime longing and the love of home, as do Mole's adventures. Instead, Diamond is the uncompromised expression of the Romantic visionary child. Wordsworth writes that a "little Child, [is] yet glorious in the might/ Of heaven-born freedom" ("Ode," 121-2). He describes himself, as a child, as lost in the ideal world:

> I was often unable to think of external things as having external existence, and I communed with all that I saw as something not apart from, but inherent in, my own immaterial nature. Many times while going to school have I grasped at a wall or tree to recall myself from this abyss of idealism to the reality. (Introduction, "Ode," 353)

He believes his own experiences to be universal: "To that dreamlike vividness and splendor which invest objects of sight in childhood, everyone, I believe, if he would look back, could bear testimony" (Introduction, "Ode," 188).

Wordsworth divides the pure child from the fallen adult, privileging the child; in "My Heart Leaps Up," he states: "The Child is father to the man." He writes of his own split, as an adult, from a "thoughtless" but more intense youthful visionary power:

> I cannot paint
> What then I was. The sounding cataract
> Haunted me like a passion: the tall rock,
> The mountain, and the deep and gloomy wood,
> Their colours and their forms, were then to me
> An appetite; a feeling and a love. . . .

> That time is past,
> And all its aching joys are now no more,
> And all its dizzy raptures. ("Tintern," 75-85)

Although Wordsworth does claim for himself, as an adult, "abundant recompense," he clearly envies a child like Diamond who still owns those dizzy raptures, whose heart still leaps up in joy of beauty.

MacDonald followed Wordsworth in privileging the visionary in childhood. The narrator of *At the Back of the North Wind* writes that a true child is "given to metaphysics" (69). He comments of Diamond in particular:

> The whole ways and look of the child, so full of quiet wisdom, . . .took hold of my heart, and I felt myself wonderfully drawn towards him. It seemed to me, somehow, as if little Diamond possessed the secret of life, and was himself what he was so ready to think the lowest living thing—an angel of God with something special to say or do. (ch. 35; 305)

Diamond moves easily between worlds, conflating real and imagined, under the guidance of his spirit-guide North Wind. She teaches him to be fearless of the world of the spirit, overcoming the apprehension and "trembling oars" Wordsworth experienced in his childhood visions. In one scene late in *At the Back of the North Wind*, the narrator relates meeting with Diamond and asking him about something he had just done for two other children:

> "What did the boy and girl want with you Diamond?" I asked.
> "They had seen a creature which frightened them."
> "And they came to see you about it?"
> "They couldn't get water out of the well for it. So they wanted me to go with them."
> "They're both bigger than you."
> "Yes, but they were frightened at it."
> "And weren't you frightened at it?"
> "No."
> "Why?"
> "Because I'm silly. I'm never frightened at things."
> I could not help thinking of the old meaning of the word *silly*. (ch. 35; 303)

The critic Eric S. Rabkin explicates the "old meaning" of Diamond as "silly" and "simple":

Although *silly* means frivolous now, it once indicated approximately the common ground between *blessed* and *innocent*. We see the same ambivalence in a word like *simple*, which can mean either *pure*, and hence *powerful* ("a simple truth"), or *mentally deficient*. By one perspective, a simple, silly, childlike innocence fulfills the gospels. (102)

In the gospel of Matthew 19:14, "Jesus said, Suffer little children, and forbid them not, to come unto me: for of such is the kingdom of heaven." In Mark 10:15, the gospels state: "Verily I say unto you, Whosoever shall not receive the kingdom of God as a little child, he shall not enter therein." These texts reveal the ancient tradition, the Christian notion that the innocent shall inherit heaven, which supports and leads to the notion of the Romantic visionary child.

Simple and silly as an angel, Diamond puts his trust in North Wind completely, even as he struggles to understand her and her enigmatic actions, which seem at times cruel or aimless. She is all-powerful, "towering up to the place of the clouds. Her hair went streaming out from her, till it spread like a mist over the stars. She flung herself abroad in space" (ch. 4; 37). But she also, in diminutive form, "helps a bee escape from a tulip," commenting: "I don't look after bees. I had this one to look after" (ch. 5; 52). She "sweeps" London out, calling it "one of my rooms" (ch. 4; 36). She brings forth a storm, her hair unwinding into the universe:

In parts indeed he could not tell which was hair and which was black storm and vapour. It seemed sometimes that all the great billows of mist-muddy wind were woven out of the crossing lines of North Wind's infinite hair, sweeping in endless intertwistings. (ch. 6; 64)

Most disturbingly of all for Diamond's faith, North Wind says she has to sink a ship, drowning all the people on board. Diamond protests that she cannot possibly be cruel. She agrees:

"No; I could not be cruel if I would. I can do nothing cruel, although I often do what looks like cruel to those who do not know what I am really doing. The people they say I drown, I only carry away to—to—to—well, the back of the North Wind—that is what they used to call it long ago, only *I* never saw the place."

"How can you carry them there if you never saw it?"

"I know the way."

"But how is it you never saw it?"

"Because it is behind me."

"But you can look round."

"Not far enough to see my own back. No; I always look before me. In fact, I grow quite blind and deaf when I try to see my back. I only mind my work."

"But how does it be your work?"

"Ah, that I can't tell you. I only know it is, because when I do it I feel all right, and when I don't I feel all wrong. East Wind says—only one does not exactly know how much to believe of what she says, for she is very naughty sometimes—she says it is all managed by a baby; but whether she is good or naughty when she says that, I don't know. I just stick to my work. It is all one to me to let a bee out of a tulip, or to sweep the cobwebs from the sky." (ch. 5; 52-3)

The things of this world do not signify in MacDonald's work; one cannot tell what matters by its seeming importance according to the terms of this world: neither size, nor fairness, nor cruelty matters. Whether North Wind must commit a slight kindness or a terrible cruelty—the saving of a bee caught in a tulip or the sinking of a ship—she must place her faith in another world, another measure. All the things she must do are but one in God's purposes.

North Wind is revealed here to be, though powerful, only an agent of the divine. She does not understand her work any more than Diamond, but she puts her faith in another, a divine child, the Christ child, and knows he, in his wisdom, knows what is right. She knows what feels right to her. North Wind is tearing Diamond away, through faith, from understanding things in terms of the external world toward a "true" or divine understanding. She is Wordsworth's "correspondent breeze" made into an actual presence and given personality.

When Diamond later on objects again to her sinking of the ship, saying, "Here you are taking care of a poor little boy with one arm, and there you are sinking a ship with the other. It can't be like you" (ch. 6; 60-1). North Wind explains that she is the same entity she was before, and that what seems evil is only the best form good could take at a specific moment. This lesson is reinforced by the moral of an interpolated fairy tale, told at an orphanage during Diamond's realistic adventures: "I never knew of any interference on the part of a wicked fairy that did not turn out a good thing in the end" (ch. 28; 228).

When Diamond asks North Wind, "how can you bear it," meaning the cruelty she must commit, she says she can bear it because of

the sound of a far-off song. I do not know exactly where it is or what it means; and I don't hear much of it, only the odour of its music. (ch. 7; 65-6)

She says the far off song

"tells me that all is right; that it is coming to swallow up all cries."
"But that won't do them any good--the people, I mean," persisted Diamond.
"It must. It must," said North Wind hurriedly. "It wouldn't be the song it seems to be if it did not swallow up all fear and pain too, and set them singing it themselves with the rest." (66)

North Wind, in describing to Diamond the "far-off song" she hears, is revealing the promise of a deeper harmony that belies all the seeming chaos. As far as North Wind can remember, the "song has been coming nearer and nearer" (66) all the time, heralding, perhaps, a coming peace or a reckoning day when the living and the dead, the worlds of matter and spirit, shall merge into one.

Diamond, a low-born child, poor and simple, is being taught by North Wind that, as Wordsworth writes, his "exterior semblance doth belie/ . . . [his] Soul's immensity" ("Ode," 108-9). As his name suggests, Diamond is something pure and precious. But a boy in this world, he is luminous in the world of the spirit. North Wind objects to the piece of paper posted over the hole into Diamond's hayloft because she uses it as "her window" to see him in his glory. When Diamond suggests she look instead into the house of a rich neighbor, North Wind is nonplussed, commenting: "Nobody makes a window into an ash-heap" (ch. 1; 11).

In *At the Back of the North Wind*, rich or poor does not matter; greatness is measured not in terms of money, but in a nobility of soul. The narrator comments:

all emperors are not gentlemen, and all cooks are not ladies—nor all queens and princesses for that matter, either. (ch. 2; 20)

Diamond's realistic adventures in a poverty-stricken London only serve to affirm, in the end, that things are not what they seem. After all, Diamond's protest to the "far-off song"—that it won't do the suffering any good in the present—could be made not only for those drowning at sea, but also for the lower-class people in MacDonald's London who suffer hardship and deprivation. Diamond himself starves, as does his family. But hardship, in MacDonald's works, only helps loosen the hold of this fallen world and reveal the world of the spirit. The critic Sheila Egoff notes:

MacDonald observes; he does not preach social reform, but his views are clear nonetheless: birth has nothing to do with character or with one's real place in life. North Wind tells Diamond: "Every man ought to be a gentleman and your father is one," and Nanny: "might have had a lady and a gentleman for a father and mother." Mr. Coleman and Mr. Raymond, who befriend Diamond and Nanny, are treated gently, but for the rich in general, MacDonald has little use. (55)

In another of MacDonald children's fantasies, *The Princess and Curdie*, the wise woman figure, a spirit-helper parallel to the matronly North Wind, tells Peter, the father of Curdie, the hero of the book:

you have got to thank me that you are so poor, Peter. I have seen to that, and it has done well for both you and me, my friend. Things come to the poor that can't get in at the door of the rich. Their money somehow blocks it up. It is a great privilege to be poor, Peter. . . . You must not mistake, however, and think it a virtue; it is but a privilege, and one also that, like other privileges, may be terribly misused. Had you been rich, my Peter, you would not have been so good as some rich men I know. (ch. 7; 53)

This speech concludes with the common revelation of the "good" but poor folk in MacDonald's children's works—that the poor are the true nobility:

And now I am going to tell you what no one knows but myself: you, Peter, and your wife both have the blood of the royal family in your veins. I have been trying to cultivate your family tree, every branch of which is known to me, and I expect Curdie to turn out a blossom on it. (ch. 7; 53)

MacDonald does not simply divorce individual character and greatness of spirit from wealth, but positively links poverty and the possibility of goodness. MacDonald's portrayal of poverty seems glib, but was born of hard experience, and perhaps a desire to find a purpose in his own distress:

Through MacDonald's long life he knew firsthand the hardships and embarrassments of poverty, the pain and depression of disease, and the heartache caused by the deaths of loved ones. (Hein, xi)

MacDonald transformed suffering, in his works, into faith, into a means towards a deeper understanding of the world of the spirit and towards right action. The reaction of the individual to suffering mattered a great deal in MacDonald's view of things. The critic Rolland Hein describes MacDonald's

strong confidence in the purpose of God to overrule all evil and recompense all suffering. But MacDonald also saw man not as a passive beneficiary of this process but as a co-creator, enlisted by God to have a large share in the creative process whereby good is realized. (1)

The individual is a co-creator through right action. Suffering can rouse the individual to a new awareness, but action must back insight if heaven is to be reached. Diamond's realistic adventures show him not only as a "true gentleman" born of a good heart, but as behaving like one. His right actions transfigure the suffering of his family and others, drawing North Wind to him and leading him back of the north wind to the river that sings "the far-off song."

MacDonald describes fairy tales in general as a means to rouse the reader, making North Wind's rousing of Diamond a metaphor for the effect of fairy stories upon readers in general, the opening of possibility that requires the reader's participation in the creative process of spiritual growth. MacDonald writes of fairy tales: "It is there not so much to convey a meaning as to wake a meaning" ("Fantastic Imagination," 317). He expands on that comment:

A fairytale is not an allegory. There may be allegory in it, but it is not an allegory. He must be an artist indeed who can, in any mode, produce a strict allegory that is not a weariness to the spirit. (317)

A fairy tale should not work on the conscious, but on the unconscious, not using allegory and reason, but emotional or spiritual understanding:

The best way [to read a fairy tale] is not to bring the forces of our intellect to bear upon it, but to be still and let it work on that part of us for whose sake it exists. (321-2)

MacDonald also writes:

The best thing you can do for your fellow, next to rousing his conscience, is—not to give him things to think about, but to wake things up that are in him; or say, to make him think things for himself. (319)

In MacDonald's fairy writings, one is to be awakened or aroused to an awareness of the revealed world of the spirit everywhere around.

This awareness, born of revelation and right action, is expressed through heightened, or in Blakean terms, "cleansed," senses. For example, a "true" or "better," or at least new, kind of hearing is necessary for Diamond to hear the "far-off song" and not simply the cries of the suffering. In MacDonald's *The Princess and Curdie*, the boy-hero Curdie gains the startling ability to feel, when he shakes hands with someone, the "true" shapes of others: sometimes he feels snake skin instead of a human hand, sometimes a human hand instead of an animal's paw, sometimes something in between. As the mystical wise woman of that book explains, "Shapes are only dresses, Curdie, and dresses are only names. That which is inside is the same all the time" (ch. 7; 54).

In *At the Back of the North Wind*, North Wind tells Diamond:

If you see me with my face all black, don't be frightened. If you see me flapping wings like a bat's, as big as the whole sky, don't be frightened. If you hear me raging ten times worse than Mrs. Bill, the blacksmith's wife—even if you see me looking in at people's windows like Mrs. Eve Dropper, the gardener's wife—you must believe that I am doing my work.

Nay, Diamond, if I change into a serpent or a tiger, you must not let go your hold of me, for my hand will never change in yours if you keep a good hold. If you keep a hold, you will know who I am all the time, even when you look at me and can't see me the least like North Wind. I may look something very awful. Do you understand? (ch. 1; 17)

Two incompatible worlds lie side by side, and the visionary must learn which of his perceptions, which senses, to trust—how to interpret the "right" touch from the "wrong" image. This kind of interpretation of a bewildering array of physical and spiritual stimuli requires Diamond to move away from this world, becoming somewhat deaf to the cries of the suffering so that he might hear the chorus of heaven. North Wind's need for absolute authority and trust becomes clear, if the awful or monstrous must be accepted without fear as the best form of the greatest good.

Perhaps the primary metaphor in MacDonald's writings for the spiritual awareness of the enlightened is imaginative sight. Wordsworth writes how "with an eye made quiet by the power/ of harmony and the deep power of joy,/ We see into the life of things" ("Tintern Abbey," 47-9). The eye of sense must be made quiet, or be cleansed, and another eye open into the world of the spirit. Like the believer looking at the humble figure of Christ, like the prince looking at Cinderella in her party dress, one must see the true heart of the matter with the eye of the spirit.

MacDonald, writing on the effect of Wordsworth's poetry, affirms: "There is not a form that lives in the world, but is a window cloven through the blank nothingness, to let us look into the heart, and feeling, and nature of God" ("Wordsworth's Poetry," 258). The imagination, the eye of the imagination, allows one to see into the heart of God, and that is not only a function of the imagination but its purpose. MacDonald states: "To inquire into what God has made is the main function of the imagination" ("The Imagination," 2).

In *The Princess and the Goblin*, the boy-hero Curdie cannot even see the wise woman, the princess Irene's grandmother, until he learns to see "aright," that is, with a more perceptive faculty than his eyes, with his imagination. Irene leads Curdie up a flight of hidden steps to the home of the matronly spirit-helper. Irene runs and sits in her grandmother's lap, but Curdie sees nothing.

He was standing in the middle of the floor looking strangely bewildered. This she [Irene] thought came of his astonishment at the beauty of the lady.

"Make a bow to my grandmother, Curdie," she said.

"I don't see any grandmother," answered Curdie rather gruffly.

"Don't see my grandmother, when I'm sitting in her lap?" exclaimed the princess.

"No, I don't," reiterated Curdie, in an offended tone.

"Don't you see the lovely fire of roses—white ones amongst them this time?" asked Irene almost as bewildered as he.

"No. I don't," answered Curdie, almost sulkily.

"Nor the blue bed? Nor the rose-colored counterpane? Nor the beautiful light, like the moon, hanging from the roof?"

"You're making a game of me, Your Royal Highness; and after what we have come through together this day, I don't think it is kind of you," said Curdie, feeling very much hurt.

"Then what do you see?" asked Irene, who perceived at once that for her not to believe him was at least as bad as for him not to believe her.

"I see a big, bare garret-room. . . . I see a tub, and a heap of musty straw, and a withered apple, and a ray of sunlight coming through the roof and shining on your head, and making all the place a curious dusky brown." (150-1)

The split between physical sight and imaginative sight is not a simple split between material and spiritual, for the eye of the imagination can also reveal false and terrible images to the foolish or impoverished in soul. In *The Princess and Curdie*, Irene's grandmother, when she came to Curdie in the mines, explains:

For instance, if a thief were to come in here just now, he would think he saw the demon of the mine, all in green flames, come to protect her treasure, and would run like a hunted wild goat. I should be all the same, but his evil eyes would see me as I am not. (ch. 7; 55)

Also, at one point in *At the Back of the North Wind*, North Wind changes herself into a wolf to frighten "a nurse that was calling a child bad names, and telling her she was wicked" (ch. 3; 34). North Wind chooses a wolf because "that was growing to be her [the nurse's] own shape inside of her" (35). Most surprising of all, North Wind reveals the disturbing truth that even Diamond does not see her as she truly is:

"I don't think I am just what you fancy me to be. I have to shape myself various ways for various people. But the heart of me is true. People call me by dreadful names, and think they know all about me. But they don't. Sometimes they call me Bad Fortune, sometimes Evil Chance, sometimes Ruin; and they have another name for me which they think most dreadful of all."

"What is that?" asked Diamond, smiling up into her face.

"I won't tell you that name." (320)

The hidden name, of course, is death, but a death that will not be named; or rather, it will be renamed as a journey back of the north wind.

In MacDonald's work, the correspondent breeze leading toward the harmony of inner and outer, or outer and beyond, at its extreme reveals itself as oblivion, as the total loss of the physical world. The sublime moment requires self-effacement into the universal; the fear in the sublime moment expresses the individual's fear of loss of identity, a fear surpassed by Diamond, or rather, mastered by North Wind. In death, there is no identity. Diamond gives himself over completely to the sublime moment, and so gives himself up completely into death. Diamond is often ill and wanes and waxes, always close to death just as he is close to the visionary. Rolland Hein comments of the spiritual in MacDonald's work:

self-abnegation, together with purity of heart and a child-like spirit of confidence and wonder in the presence of the universal mystery of things, is necessary to achieve the desired oneness with God. (xi)

Likewise, Wordsworth writes of the "sublime" as:

> that blessed mood
> In which the burthen of the mystery,
> In which the heavy and the weary weight
> Of all this unintelligible world
> Is lightened:--that serene and blessed mood,
> in which the affections gently lead us on,--
> Until, the breath of this corporeal frame
> And even the motion of our human blood
> Almost suspended, we are laid asleep
> In body, and become a living soul. ("Tintern," 37-46)

That death will not reveal its name is significant, for when named it is final; the death North Wind offers equivocates itself as a life-in-death, a "living soul" that is "asleep in body."

In MacDonald's powerful short story "The Golden Key," a young boy, Mossy, finds a golden key at the end of rainbow, a hint of the transcendent world of the spirit, and goes on a spiritual quest. On his journey, he meets a girl, Tangle. Together and separately, they travel beyond the rainbow to the country where the shadows lie, into death.

> "You have tasted of death, now," said the Old Man. "Is it good?"
> "It is good," said Mossy. "It is better than life."
> "No," said the Old Man: "it is only more life." (68)

In his first visit to the land back of the north wind, Diamond falls deathly ill in life and North Wind leads him, perhaps in a dream, to the very north, to what North Wind calls her "doorstep," where she herself, transparent, nearly nonexistent, sits without moving. She tells Diamond to travel through her.

When he reached her knees, he put out his hand to lay it on her; but nothing was there save an intense cold. He walked on. Then all grew white about him; and the cold stung him like fire. He walked on still, groping through the whiteness. It thickened about him. At last, it got into his heart, and he lost all sense. I would say that he fainted—only whereas in common faints all grows black about you, he felt swallowed up in whiteness. It was when he reached North Wind's heart that he fainted and fell. But as he fell, he rolled over the threshold, and it was thus that Diamond got to the back of the north wind. (ch. 9; 95)

Back of the north wind, Diamond finds no sun, just "a certain still rayless light," which Diamond thought "came out of the flowers" (ch. 10; 99). He finds the river which made the far-off music: "in the troubles which followed, Diamond was often heard singing; and when asked what he was singing, would answer: "'One of the tunes the river at the back of the north wind sung'" (99). Overall, he feels a great peace: "so still and quiet and patient and contented, that, as far as the mere feeling went, it was something better than mere happiness" (99). In "The Golden Key," Tangle, in the presence of the Old Man of Fire, had a marvelous sense that she was in the secret of the earth and all its ways. Everything she had seen, or learned from books; all that her grandmother had said or sung to her; all the talk of the beasts, birds and fishes . . . all was plain: she understood it all, and saw that everything meant the same thing, though she could not have put it into words again. (59)

Diamond returned from the world of the spirit, although only for a brief time, because of an uncharacteristic feeling of longing for home brought on by the sight of "his mother crying" (ch. 11; 101) (and perhaps the necessity of plot, which required Diamond to tell his story to the narrator). As in other descriptions of the sublime, Diamond experiences a divine forgetfulness when he falls out of the universal: "when he came back, he had forgotten a great deal, and what he did remember was very hard to tell" (ch. 10; 96). Diamond thinks he has been gone years and years but North Wind tells him it was only seven days (ch. 11; 104). His mother tells him he has been sick, and she thought him dead. But, despite his loss of memory, something abides. The narrator asks Diamond:

"Do you want to go back again?"
"No: I don't think I have ever left it. I feel it here somewhere." (ch. 9; 101)

MacDonald describes just such a feeling of the spirit as immanent in all things in Wordsworth's poetry: "The very element in which the mind of Wordsworth lived and moved was a Christian pantheism" ("Wordsworth's Poetry," 245), the "belief that God is in everything, and showing himself in everything" (246). Thus, MacDonald's work also expresses a belief that the world of the spirit is in everything, and shows itself everywhere. MacDonald expands on his comments of Wordsworth as the poet of God in nature:

Wordsworth is the high priest of nature thus regarded. He saw God present everywhere; not always immediately, in his own form, it is true; but whether he looked upon the awful mountain-peak, sky-encompassed with loveliness, or upon the face of a little child, which is as it were eyes in the face of nature—in all things he felt the solemn presence of the Divine Spirit. ("Wordsworth's Poetry," 247)

MacDonald's work presents a Wordsworthian view of childhood as well. In the terms of the Wordsworthian child, adulthood is failure. Similarly, Diamond, if he is to succeed as a visionary, cannot grow up. He must die a joyful, perfect death into the sublime moment. And his death must be more than death. Wordsworth writes:

I used to brood over the stories of Enoch and Elijah, and almost to persuade myself that, whatever may become of others, I should be translated, in something of the same way, to heaven. (Introduction, "Ode," 353)

Diamond is translated into the world of the spirit through a death that is life. The narrator of *At the Back of the North Wind*, in the last lines of the book, after Diamond dies, declares of Diamond: "They thought he was dead. I knew that he had gone to the back of the north wind" (ch. 38; 332). Diamond dies happily into a living soul, and experiences the fantastic sublime in an absolute way. The imaginative experience of the fantastic sublime in MacDonald's work not only presents the impossible or divine in actual form, but moves Diamond into the world of the imagination itself, into glory, into an absolute subjectivity that denies death in the face of death.

Diamond's early death reveals a disturbing underside to the fantastic sublime as it played out in some nineteenth-century children's literature. The sublime adventures of Tom, the little chimney sweeper in Charles Kingsley's *Water Babies* (1863), practically begins with his early death by drowning, after which he becomes a water baby, a living spirit, for the balance of the book. Oscar Wilde's Christ child in "The Selfish Giant" (1888) is also sentimentalized by an appropriately early death. The phenomenon of the precious child fit only for death is evident in realistic nineteenth-century children's literature as well, in works, for example, by Dickens and Alcott. Indeed, the problem is not at the heart of the fantastic sublime, but at the heart of the fictional realization of the Wordsworthian child, which can only be, at the least, problematic, and at the worst, exploitive.

The Romantic sublime was always explicitly located in adulthood, a fallen adulthood, which longed for childhood and the return to the visionary from which it was ultimately isolated and alienated. The natural sublime, grounded in nature, expressed the adult's attachment to this world; the sublime moment always balanced the sudden apprehension of the visionary—of childhood—with the impossibility of maintaining the visionary and, finally, regret and sweet longing. The fantastic sublime in MacDonald's work, and in some other nineteenth-century children's fantasies, relocated the sublime moment into childhood itself, where the undifferentiated soul can fully grasp the visionary. Yet children's fantasy must implicitly come from an adult perspective. Adults must, after all, write, read and buy children's literature. The fantastic sublime realized in the *puer aeternus*, the divine child, becomes not only an attempt to relate the sublime moment, but to recapture it and repackage it, to control it and own it. The fantastic sublime of the early death of children expresses an adult longing for childhood, which has moved beyond the sentimental into a possession and restriction where joy becomes death.

As Part III of this work will show, the control of childhood expressed by their joyful early deaths has implications for women, for those who are not allowed to claim authority in society. The most famous writers of nineteenth-century children's fantasy literature were overwhelmingly male even as the majority of writers of nineteenth-century children's literature were overwhelmingly female. In Part III, Christina Rossetti's fantasy *Goblin Market* will be read as a critique of the fantastic sublime from the perspective not of the wistful adult male, but the controlled other—a female as child—who is expected to remain in innocence or die happily, but never to grow up.

CHRISTINA ROSSETTI'S GOBLIN MARKET AND THE FEMININE REREADING OF THE FANTASTIC SUBLIME

Chapter 9

The Price of Fairy Fruit in *Goblin Market*

At the beginning of Christina Rossetti's *Goblin Market*, the two sisters Laura and Lizzie, like Diamond and like Mole, hear voices calling from beyond the world. As Diamond hears North Wind demanding to be let in, and as Mole, called from his whitewashing, hears a mystic voice in the wind in the willows, so the two sisters are called from their domestic chores, as "They went with pitchers to the reedy brook" (22) to fetch water, by persistent magic voices at twilight, "Evening by evening/ Among the brookside rushes" (6). But the voices Laura and Lizzie hear are neither the motherly North Wind nor the "Friend and Helper" Pan; instead, Laura and Lizzie hear the seductive cry of the goblin merchant men selling fairy fruit: "Come buy, come buy" (3). If Mole and Diamond had to pay for their spiritual seeking, Mole abandoning and almost losing his home, that "anchorage in one's existence," and experiencing the Terror of the Wild Wood, and Diamond giving up his life, his adult life, for the world of the spirit, the price remained unstated at purchase.

Christina Rossetti's explicit introduction of goblin merchants, of a commerce with the other world, a barter for the sublime, reveals her emphasis on the price to be paid for longing and desire. Diamond knew his death led to a place of wonder and love. Mole and Rat knew that the sublime wind in the willows promised joy, and that if they only acted wisely they might avoid the dangers and fragmentation of the failed sublime. Laura and Lizzie, in contrast, have no assurances, only the desire for the transcendent and its queer and terrible sellers. The goblin men and their fairy fruit bring the rapture of the sublime, but only at a price.

Goblin Market posits two separate worlds. First, there is the daylight domestic world of home and hearth where the sisters perform their chores

> like bees, as sweet and busy:
> Laura rose with Lizzie:
> Fetched in honey, milked the cows,
> Aired and set to rights the house,
> Kneaded cakes of whitest wheat,
> Cakes for dainty mouths to eat,
> Next churned butter, whipped up cream,
> Fed their poultry, sat and sewed. (21-2)

The other world is found at night in the "haunted glen" (52) of the goblin men. The two worlds meet on the riverbank where the women go to fetch water; and, at twilight, the goblin merchant men come to open goblin market and sell their magic fruit. Each sister goes to goblin market and attempts to buy the wares of the merchant men, leaving, like Mole with his whitewashing, the domestic world behind; the contrasts and lessons of the two sisters' separate attempts to realize the ecstasy of the fairy fruit comment on the dangers, pleasures and possibilities of the fantastic sublime, the realization of joy "beyond the walls of the world," from a particularly feminine position, which unmasks the promise of the sublime as (unwittingly) gendered male.

Unsurprisingly, the goblin's fruits, unknown and supernatural, are, for Laura and Lizzie at least, both dangerous and forbidden. As Laura says before her encounter with the goblins: "We must not buy their fruits:/ Who knows upon what soil they fed/ their hungry thirsty roots?" (7). Yet Laura looks at the goblin men even as she warns against looking: "'Lie close,' Laura said,/ Pricking up her golden head: 'We must not look at goblin men'" (7). As Lizzie implores her, "Laura, Laura,/ You should not peep at goblin men" (7), Laura wonders aloud: "How fair the vine must grow/ Whose grapes are so luscious;/

How warm the wind must blow/ Through those fruit bushes" (7-10).

Fear and desire dance around one another, as in the opening of the second phase of the sublime, when the normal, habitual—one might say, domestic—relationship of objects suddenly breaks down and is replaced by an indeterminate relationship, a disconcerting disproportion between inner and outer, and with overwhelming feelings, mixed feelings of wonder and anxiety.

The appearance of many goblin men, of multiple fantastic figures as contrasted to the unity of the one helper-spirit, Pan or North Wind, in the works of Grahame and MacDonald, marks the fantastic in Rossetti's work as taking part in the blockage of the sublime moment. In the arrest of the second phase of Weiskel's structure of the sublime, the promise of joy is frustrated either through lack or, as with the description of the goblin men, through overabundance—strange image following image—which overwhelms:

> One had a cat's face,
> One whisked a tail.
> One tramped a rat's pace
> One crawled like a snail,
> One like a wombat prowled obtuse and furry,
> One like a ratel tumbled hurry skurry. (10)

Only one element of each figure is described, leaving the goblins, in effect, undescribed, only half-seen, unknown even as regarded face-to-face, making the fantastic figures of the goblins take part, in some strange way, of both the lack *and* the overabundance of the blockage of the sublime. The images used to describe the goblins are not grotesque, but neither are they comfortable: the animals are familiar and small, but the idea of a man-shaped thing crawling up to one like a snail, for example, is odd, even disquieting.

The multiple voices of the merchant men, like their multiple cry "come buy, come buy," are also disconcerting and difficult to read. A crowd of merchants and only one customer makes goblin market a tangle of enticing utterances, a babble beyond one's ability to respond to all at once:

> The whisk-tailed merchant bade her taste
> In tones as smooth as honey,

> The cat-faced purr'd,
> The rat-paced spoke a word
> Of welcome, and the snail-paced even was heard;
> One parrot-voiced and jolly
> Cried "Pretty Goblin" still for "Pretty Polly;"—
> One whistled like a bird. (14-5)

The goblins' over-friendly voices put one on guard as one waits for the merchant men to set the price on their "forbidden," black market wares:

> She heard a voice like voice of doves
> Cooing all together:
> They sounded kind and full of loves
> In the pleasant weather. (10)

The phrase "In the pleasant weather" implies that their voices will sound different in "unpleasant" weather, or even when the weather just is not "pleasant" enough for fair-weather friends. The soothing quality of the goblins' voices "full of love" is undermined by their constant secret communication of "leering" looks and "sly" movements of hand and body:

> When they reached where Laura was
> They stood stock still upon the moss,
> Leering at each other,
> Brother with queer brother;
> Signalling each other,
> Brother with sly brother. (14)

The community of "sly brothers" is set in opposition to the loving sisters. One waits for the secret communication to reveal itself as not love but seduction and betrayal—for the price to be set and for it to be too high.

The overabundance of different kinds of fairy fruit in the cry of the goblin men, the gorgeous description, rich in language as in tastes, is also ultimately beyond knowing, beyond eating and tasting all at once, an exhausting multiplication of desires:

Come buy our orchard fruits,
Come buy, come buy:
Apples and quinces,
Lemons and oranges,
Plump unpecked cherries,
Melons and raspberries,
Bloom-down-cheeked peaches,
Swart-headed mulberries,
Wild free-born cranberries,
Crab-apples, dewberries,
Pine-apples, blackberries,
Apricots, strawberries;—
All ripe together
In summer weather,—
Morns that pass by,
Fair eves that fly;
Come buy, come buy:
Our grapes fresh from the vine,
Pomegranates full and fine,
Dates and sharp bullaces,
Rare pears and greengages,
Damsons and bilberries,
Taste them and try:
Currants and gooseberries,
Bright-fire-like barberries,
Figs to fill your mouth,
Citrons from the South,
Sweet to tongue and sound to eye;
Come buy, come buy. (3-6)

These exotic, impossible fruits, which could not in reality be "all ripe together in summer weather," are a feast of the imagination, beyond realization. All the proffered fruits could not be eaten at once without the mouth deadening to so many rare tastes, without the stomach bursting. "Men sell not such in any town" is the constant refrain of the poem, emphasizing that the fruits, although with names of real, often exotic, fruits, are not real but something from the world of imagination. As the critic Jeanie Watson writes:

The cry of the goblin men is almost hypnotic in its rich catalogue of fruits so numerous as to be virtually unending. The kinds and quantities and combinations of taste and color are unlimited, appealing to the senses and to the possibilities of the imagination. ("Christina Rossetti," 70)

Rather, the fairy fruits appeal to the impossibilities of the imagination, to what cannot be grasped and held, "suggestive of infinity" as Coleridge writes of sublime misty mountaintops.

Laura longs for the fruit of the goblin merchant men but has no money; the goblins finally set their price: "'You have much gold upon your head.'/ They answered all together" (17), "all together" as if that had been the price all along, agreed upon by the "sly" brotherhood through secret signal. Laura pays the price and eats the fruit:

> She clipped a precious golden lock,
> She dropped a tear more rare than pearl,
> Then sucked their fruit globes fair or red:
> Sweeter than honey from the rock,
> Stronger than man-rejoicing wine,
> Clearer than water flowed that juice;
> She never tasted such before,
> How should it cloy with length of use?
> She sucked and sucked and sucked the more
> Fruits which that unknown orchard bore;
> She sucked until her lips were sore;
> Then flung the rinds away
> But gathered up one kernel-stone,
> And knew not was it night or day
> As she turned home alone. (17)

Laura's experience is astonishing: What has been paid and what has been gained? The meaning of the fantastic images open and close. The rapture, where Laura "knew not was it night or day," is clear, the beauty of the moment captured in the beauty of the language is fully realized, full with passion, but not easily understood. The experience is, at first reading, obviously sexual. As the critic Janet Casey writes:

Most critics have quickly identified these goblins with eroticism: their fruits, an obvious reference to the Eve story, are described in sensual terms (e.g., "Plump, unpecked cherries," "Bloom-down-cheeked peaches," "Pomegranates full and fine"); the goblins have seductive voices, sounding "kind and full of loves" and with "tones as smooth as honey"; when Laura eats their fruits there is a marked repetition of the word "sucked." Laura has to pay for the goblins' fruits with part of her body, Lizzie is physically molested by the goblins, and the fate of Jeanie, "Who should have been a bride;/ But who for joys brides hope to have/ Fell sick and died," is also apparently related to the goblins' carnal nature. These lascivious creatures most certainly represent the lure of erotic love. (66)

Moreover, the use of images with obvious sexual meaning, the expression of the striving of desire, is evident in Rossetti's description of Laura straining to see the "forbidden" goblin men tramping into the haunted glen:

> Laura stretched her gleaming neck
> Like a rush-imbedded swan,
> Like a lily from the beck,
> Like a moonlit poplar branch.
> Like a vessel at the launch
> When its last restraint is gone. (11)

However, the poetry oversails: the sexuality becomes, just as clearly, something more—a desire for the intense experience of imagination, an experience both revealed in and co-mingled with sexual love. As the critic Sylvia Bailey Shurbutt comments:

Rossetti's lines pulsate not only with sexual implication but with the suggestion that Laura's hunger, her oral craving, goes beyond mere sexual fulfillment; the hunger here is also for knowledge and creative expression, for poetic articulation as well as carnality. (41)

Indeed, Laura describes the fruit to Lizzie as joy "Too huge for me to hold," telling her:

> Have done with sorrow;
> I'll bring you plumbs to-morrow
> Fresh on their mother twigs,
> Cherries worth getting;
> You cannot think what figs
> My teeth have met in,
> What melons icy-cold

> Piled on a dish of gold
> Too huge for me to hold,
> What peaches with a velvet nap,
> Pellucid without one seed:
> Odorous indeed must be the mead
> Whereon they grow, pure the wave they drink
> With lilies at the brink,
> And sugar sweet their sap. (19-20)

Laura's experience with the fairy fruit is at the same time intimately tied to the physical and beyond the physical, too "pure," too much, too rich to be physical joy alone.

The sexuality of Laura's experience is tied up with the distinct gendering of the twin worlds of home and haunted glen—the female home and the male glen. The goblin men are not androgynous but male, and yet they are not men—"Men sell not such [fruits] in any town"—but gendered fantastic figures who, in turn, gender the fantastic sublime moment, and so gender the experience of the pleasures of the imagination and complicate Laura's attempt to realize those pleasures. Laura's seeking runs afoul of Rossetti's polarized gender roles, and suggests Laura is looking for something beyond her prescribed place in the roles of the sexes:

The goblin men are purveyors not only of sexual liberation and bacchanal pleasures but of creative liberation as well; they hold the keys to the masculine world of creative activity and knowledge. (Shurbutt, 41)

A better metaphor might be: the goblin men of this work hold not the keys but the forbidden fruit of the masculine world of imagination. The fruit is the possibility for both spiritual sorrow and spiritual joy. After all, if the fruit did not hold some promise of desire fulfilled, Laura would not have looked. As the critic Dolores Rosenblum writes: "the villainy is so undisguised, how can she be so greedy, so monomaniacal, so obstinately blind? Set against the soul's yearning for bliss, however, Laura's longings look like—indeed are—immortal longings" (69). Laura's craving "is both a synecdoche for a full range of sensual appetites and a thirsting for the feast that is God" (90).

Laura's hunger is the hunger of the soul for the world of the spirit, for the sublime moment, realized in *Goblin Market* through the fantastic sublime of the fairy fruit, which when eaten brings a transport beyond the last restraint of the world, beyond knowing day from night—too huge to hold, sweeter than honey from the rock. However, once Laura has tasted that joy, and paid the price of lock and tear, she can no longer hear the goblin men when they come at twilight: "Laura turned cold as stone/ To find her sister heard that cry alone,/ That goblin cry,/ "Come buy our fruits, come buy" (26). The goblin world took what it wanted from Laura and now has no use for her, no concern for her continuing desire. In *Goblin Market*, the world of the imagination belongs to men, and women enter only at the pleasure of their goblin desires.

The cautionary tale of Jeanie, who "met them [the goblins] in the moonlight,/ Took their gifts both choice and many,/ Ate their fruits and wore their flowers. . . . But ever in the noonlight/ She pined and pined away;/ Sought them by night and day,/ Found them no more, but dwindled and grew gray;/ Then fell with the first snow" (18), serves to universalize Laura's tale as the plight of all women in their dealings with goblin men. How men, human men, are treated is left unstated: men might seek and find and find again the fairy fruit, might visit the unknown orchards where the fruit grows, might live forever, like Diamond, in the world of fairy; readers only know for certain that women are allowed one glimpse of joy and nothing more.

Laura thinks, at the loss of the goblin's fairy fruit, "Must she no more such succous pasture find,/ Gone deaf and blind?" (26). The fairy fruit brings true sight and hearing—the images and voices of the goblin men—the true taste of the impossibly sweet fruit, the true experience of joy, but all falls away. The kernel Laura keeps from her feast on fairy fruit symbolizes her failed attempt to bring the experience back with her into her domestic world; the seed, planted, even "Dewed . . . with tears" (29), does not grow.

Laura is "like a leaping flame" (23) after tasting the fruit, but after learning she could not hear the goblin men "She dwindled, as the fair moon doth turn/ To swift decay and burned/ Her fire away" (29) like Jeanie before her. The fruit tastes of sweetness and joy, but brings for Laura afterward only longing and a slow withering of unfulfilled desire leading toward death. Instead of divine forgetfulness characteristic of the third phase of the sublime, the recovery of the sublime moment, there is only an eternal unfulfilled desire, the abridgement of the sublime moment confined to the blockage of the second phase without end or relief.

The male and female worlds of *Goblin Market* are separate, no man ever appears in the domestic world of the sisters, and antithetical, the goblin world uses, and uses up, the women who enter. But once Laura has eaten the fruit of goblin market, she cannot fully leave the "haunted glen" behind and reenter, fully, her own world. A longing follows her and harms her. Laura crosses the division of the seperate worlds of men and women but to her detriment. After Laura's feast on goblin fruit, when she longs for the next twilight, the next goblin market and her next taste of fairy fruit—not knowing she will never hear the goblin cry again—the two sisters experience the domestic world of home in two ways, revealing Laura's inability to fully reenter the world the two sisters had once shared. As the women sit and sew, they talk:

> Lizzie with an open heart,
> Laura in an absent dream,
> One content, one sick in part;
> One warbling for the mere bright day's delight,
> One longing for the night. (22)

Home, as the proverb goes, "is where the heart is"; the "haunted glen" is an absent dream, both an absent-minded dream and a dream once held and now missing. Home is contentment; the remembrance of the glen is the sickness of longing and discontent with the world. The domestic world belongs to the day; the "haunted glen" and the merchant men belong to the night. Home is female, the glen is male.

The divided worlds of *Goblin Market* are out of balance and suffer with longing for one another. Laura's longing is well-chronicled, but the goblins, too, must desire the women with a terrible desire to come night after night, to call night after night, every night, in search of them, if only for one night's pleasure; such an existence seems lonely and strange, pathetic and hateful.

As the following chapters will show, Lizzie's encounter with the goblin men, informed by Laura's failure to realize the sublime, will come with a clearer view of the gender of the fantastic sublime, and will offer a feminine rereading of the sublime moment, a rereading that will again attempt to fuse the antithetical worlds, but with more success, presenting what might be called a *domesticated* fantastic sublime.

Chapter 10

The Domesticated Sublime in Mary Shelley's *Frankenstein*

Another nineteenth-century fantastic work, Mary Shelley's Gothic masterpiece *Frankenstein* (1818), can be read as a feminine critique of the (male) Romantic sublime, similar to the critique Laura's tale in *Goblin Market* makes of the unwitting gender of the fantastic sublime. In his monomaniacal search for the secret of life, Victor Frankenstein is like a (male) Romantic poet following the "mythopoeic vision that inspired the first generation of Romantic poets and thinkers" (Mellor, *Mary Shelley*, 70). The monster Frankenstein created is the unknown made manifest in fantastic form: "The creature thus represents the confrontation of the human mind with an unknowable nature, with the experience that eighteenth-century philosophers called the sublime" (131).

The eighteenth-century version of the sublime, drawn from hints in Longinus' and Joseph Addison's discussions of aesthetics and explored by Immanuel Kant and, perhaps most fully, by Edmund Burke in his *A Philosophical Inquiry into the Origins of Our Ideas of the Sublime and Beautiful* (1757), was the precursor of the Romantic sublime. It was predominantly concerned with what in the Romantic sublime has been called "the blockage of the sublime moment," the apprehension of the abyss.

In Burke, fear was the source of the sublime, which he specifically located in a catalogue of Gothic landscapes, lonely mountaintops, wastes and thunder storms. Such sublime landscapes appear often in *Frankenstein* and, as Mellor notes, "The appearances of the creature in the novel are simultaneous with the revelation of the [eighteenth century] sublime" (*Mary Shelley*, 131), with Gothic wastelands of snow and mountains, while the "creature himself embodies the human sublime" (132) due to his size and strength, as well as his horrible birth out of the dead matter of corpses. The monster, then, represents the failed Romantic sublime, or what might be called the Gothic or uncanny sublime of dissolution and blockage.

Weiskel divides the eighteenth-century and Romantic versions of the sublime as, respectively, "negative" and "positive." As the critic Anne Mellor explains of both sublime landscapes and Weiskel's definitions:

Burke and Kant suggested that the meaning of such an immense landscape is the infinite and incomprehensible power of God or nature (the thing-in-itself). In this reading, what is signified (divine omnipotence or the *Ding-an-sich*) is greater than the signifier (the landscape and linguistic descriptions of it). Weiskel called this the "negative" sublime, since the human mind is finally overwhelmed or negated by a greater even transcendent power. In contrast, Wordsworth in the Mount Snowden episode of *The Prelude* or Coleridge in "This Lime Tree Bower My Prison" suggested that the meaning of the sublime landscape may lie in its capacity to inspire the poetic imagination to a conception of its own power as a "mighty mind" or "almighty spirit." In this reading what is signified (the landscape) is less than the signifier (the poetic language produced by the creative imagination). Weiskel has called this the "positive" sublime, since the human mind finally confronts its own linguistic power. (*Mary Shelley*, 132)

The overwhelming nature of the eighteenth-century sublime described by Burke, and later by Immanuel Kant, has obvious connections to Weiskel's notion of the arrest of the second phase of the sublime moment without the restoration and relief of the third phase—of a failed attempt to realize the Romantic or "positive" sublime. It has connections as well to the critic David B. Morris' notion of a Gothic sublime, and to Freud's uncomfortable realization of the uncanny.

Laura's tale of loss and withering, if it ended *Goblin Market*, if Lizzie's encounter with the goblin men did not occur, would make Rossetti's work not a story of the fantastic sublime—of transcendence—but a tale of horror, a Gothic tale like *Frankenstein* or Oscar Wilde's story of moral decay, *The Picture of Dorian Gray* (1891), where the fantastic only serves to baffle and frighten, bringing blockage and horror, an unwanted insight into the ravages of desire. But Laura's tale does not end *Goblin Market*! Instead, it serves as an implicit critique of the fantastic sublime—damning it as distinctly male and as excluding, even erasing, the feminine. As Mellor comments on the Romantic sublime experience:

> It is crucial to see that the powerful pleasure produced by the experience of the sublime for both Coleridge and Wordsworth . . . rests on their capacity to erase the difference between self and other. (*Romanticism and Gender*, 89)

Mellor equates this erasure of the physical world with the erasure of the female body (88). Laura's tale in *Goblin Market* also involved the erasure of the feminine through goblin men's misuse of women, which leads to the slow withering and death of the female body.

Mary Shelley's Gothic work functions as a critique of (male) Romanticism, similar to Rossetti's critique in Laura's tale of the fantastic sublime, exposing the Romantic sublime as a failure, at least for women and/or the world of women, located in *Frankenstein*, as in *Goblin Market*, in the family and the home. The search for the sublime is shown to have a price, and a high price at that. Andrew Griffin writes:

> Mary Shelley, though intellectually a Romantic, seems almost a Victorian at heart. Her novel never questions the reality and the power of Romantic reconciliations—Frankenstein's quest is successful. . . . But it does expose the disregard for simple human needs that seems inseparably a part of all Romantic exploration. Frankenstein's Prometheanism is more and more clearly revealed as obsessive and inhuman, the cause of much suffering and many deaths. More profoundly, *Frankenstein* betrays the conviction that a knowledge of the principles of life gives us no cause to rejoice: that the elements mixed in man make for disharmony, monstrosity, and tragedy. Frankenstein's creation is a monster, after all, sublime only in his Dantean

ugliness. The Monster's narrative reveals a conservative distrust of Romantic extremes, a Victorian longing for security, society, and self-command, symbolized (as in *Jane Eyre*) by the domestic hearth. Only when he loses all hope of companionship does he run, as it were, to cold and ice; finally, in a condition of almost philosophical despair, to a "Romantic" synthesis of both in his dramatic suicide-by-fire at the North pole. (50-1)

Victor Frankenstein, in his thirst for "forbidden" knowledge, leaves his family behind to create his monster; the monster, in turn, destroys the Frankenstein family as revenge for Frankenstein's inability to be a father or mother, to love his child, or even to give him a wife—a family to love. Mellor writes of Mary Shelley:

The liberation of the imagination advocated by the Romantic poets was regarded by Mary Shelley as both promiscuous and potentially evil. (*Mary Shelley*, 137)

P.D. Fleck comments on the hubris and dangers of man's attempt to realize the divine in *Frankenstein*:

The stand the novel takes is that man's place in the universe is a fixed one; whatever creative powers he has, whatever divinity is within him, is destructive when man, like Prometheus, seeks to be a god. ("Mary Shelley's Notes," 253)

Harold Bloom adds:

Frankenstein breaks through the barrier that separates man from God and gives apparent life, but in doing so he gives only death-in-life. The profound dejection endemic in Mary Shelley's novel is fundamental to the Romantic mythology of the self, for all Romantic horrors are diseases of excessive consciousness, of the self unable to bear the self. ("Frankenstein," 127)

The horror of the blockage of the sublime moment is itself a disease of excessive consciousness, of an extreme realization of self-consciousness without relief and transcendence beyond the self, a death-in-life.

Mellor locates the feminine response to the failure of the (male) Romantic sublime in a countertradition of female poets and writers who combine the aesthetic responses to beauty and to the sublime and thereby realize a new form of the sublime. In essence, women writers of Gothic and Romance literature contemporary to the works of the Romantic poets, throw the extreme self-consciousness of Romanticism over for the love of others, for the human joy of family and community, although still with some compromised realization of the sublime, the divine, moment. Mellor writes that in the

feminine Romantic tradition, the sublime combines with the beautiful to produce, not the experience . . . of solitary, visionary transcendence sought (however futilely) by several male Romantic poets, but an experience of communion between two different people . . . [a] *domesticated* sublimity. (*Romanticism and Gender*, 103)

Rossetti's work—in the tale of Lizzie's attempt to win the goblin fruit—also counters the sublime joy offered by the goblin men with an experience of community between two people, a vision of the world of the spirit based on the love of sisters for one another, a domesticated fantastic sublime.

Chapter 11

The Imagination Unbound
in *Goblin Market*

The sisters in Christina Rossetti's *Goblin Market* are strongly identified with one another, an equality of "sisterhood" that controls the poem. Sleeping side by side, the sisters are interchangeable:

> Golden head by golden head,
> Like two pigeons in one nest
> Folded in each other's wings.
> They lay down in their curtained bed:
> Like two blossoms on one stem,
> Like two flakes of new-fall'n snow,
> Like two wands of ivory
> Tipped with gold for awful kings. (21)

They are, indeed, at times, so strongly identified as to be fused:

> Cheek to cheek and breast to breast
> Locked together in one nest. (21)

However, their actions with the goblin men are as different as, to borrow a metaphor back from Rossetti, night and day.

As noted in an earlier chapter, when the goblins first call to the sisters, Laura strives to see and hear while "Lizzie veiled her blushes" (6). Lizzie warns her sister against the goblins and then, the goblins approaching, she "thrust a dimpled finger/ In each ear, shut eyes and ran" (10) in a curious repetition of a scene from Bunyan's *Pilgrim's Progress* (1684): Christian also shuts his eyes and ears and runs away from his family, his wife and children, but he shuts out the cries of his family, the unbelievers, and runs toward the world of the spirit; Lizzie shuts out the call of the other world as she runs back home. Christian is another, early example of the world of the feminine, defined by Rossetti and Mary Shelley as home and community, left behind by man in his solitary and exclusionary pursuit of spirit. Like Christian, Laura pursues the world of the spirit with a singular purpose, but where Christian wins the Celestial City (a place, like Diamond's back of the north wind, beyond and including death), Laura is excluded from the joy of the other world, the sudden, momentary abundance of the sublime fruit being replaced by loss and lack, blockage and slow withering.

The sisters' opposite actions at the goblins' first appearance might make them appear to be, and they have been read as, two halves or two aspects of one personality. In this reading, *Goblin Market* is a Christian allegory, replaying the two central events of Christianity: humanity's temptation and fall, and, in Lizzie's rescue of her sister, humanity's redemption. Laura is Eve; Lizzie is Christ. The comparison of the poem and the biblical stories is, at first glance, apt. Laura has fallen to temptation, and Lizzie heroically saves her sister from withering away at the loss of the goblin fairy fruit by bringing home the sweet juice. At second glance, however, the poem complicates any simple Christian reading.

Goblin Market did appropriate the stories of Eve and of Christ, but a straightforward allegorical reading fails to realize the relationship of Laura and Lizzie is one of equals, "two blossoms on one stem." Lizzie is not, at least in any transparent, simplistic sense, Laura's better half, nor is Laura Lizzie's "dark side." Further, a Christian allegorical reading fails to account for each sister's growth in the poem, a growth towards one another, each sister a model for the other, each "redeeming" the other. As the critic Janet Casey notes:

Although Laura alone succumbs to the temptations of the goblin fruit, neither Lizzie not the narrator offers negative judgment of her. (68)

Laura's fall is not the shame of original sin. A Christian allegorical reading is, in essence, only half right; it interprets, successfully enough, Laura's encounter with the goblin men as a fall, but fails to read Lizzie's tale closely enough to understand it as another attempt to gain the fruit Laura had failed to obtain. Striving for the fairy fruit is not wrong, a negative act, a sin. How Laura sought the fruit may have precipitated her fall, may have been wrong, or the goblin's cruelty may be faulted, or both; but the fruit itself, its sublime juice, is good and sweet, as Lizzie proves in her encounter with the goblin men.

The fruit is described as "like honey to the throat/ But poison to the blood" (52); the critic Jeanie Watson writes of Laura and the fruit, "she had wished to divide the honey from the sting" ("Christina Rossetti," 69). Lizzie would find out how to do just that, discovering not how to resist the temptation of the goblin's fairy fruit, but how to obtain it, the sap and the sweetness, without paying the goblin's price. As Watson writes, "*Goblin Market* is an extremely subversive poem," which affirms in the end the right of the two sisters to the goblin fruit, even while warning of the dangers involved in procuring it. Watson comments:

> The stance is made possible through Rossetti's choice of form for the poem: the interplay of fairy tale and moral tale. This interplay subverts the accepted moral into the immoral and makes imaginative knowledge the only righteousness acceptable. ("Christina Rossetti," 64)

The other way of reading *Goblin Market* is as a fairy tale. In the moral tale of Christian allegory, Lizzie saved Laura; in the fairy tale, Laura is the braver soul striving for the transcendent moment of the fantastic sublime and moving Lizzie toward a world, formerly closed to her, but to which, Laura's actions imply, she has a right. The fairy tale in *Goblin Market* shows the women, each in turn, how to find their way to the world of erotic love and spiritual joy, a world that once belonged only to the goblin men, but that Lizzie, Laura's example before her, will achieve. For Watson, the two readings of *Goblin Market* as moral tale and fairy tale are at odds, and the fairy tale subverts the moral. She comments that Rossetti knew well, and employed in her writing, both the fairy tale and the moral tale:

However, the forms are essentially antithetical, one being used for didactic purposes to teach children proper spiritual and social conduct, the other being secular or amoral, or even immoral, in its lesson. ("Christina Rossetti," 65)

As the first part of this work explored, fairy tales, once appropriated by Romanticism, could also become instruments of spiritual teaching, a teaching that transfigures the "immorality" of fairy tales into a freedom and exultation of the imagination as it reaches into the world of the spirit. As the critic Bruno Bettelheim observes in *The Uses of Enchantment*:

Literary critics [and fantasists] such as G.K. Chesterson [in *Orthodoxy*] and C.S. Lewis [in *The Allegory of Love*] felt that fairy tales are "spiritual explorations" and hence "the most life-like," revealing "human life as seen, or felt, or divined from the inside." (24)

Fairy tales have a moral purpose, but one that is fundamentally at odds with the unimaginative and didactic traditional moral tale. Watson comments, that while the real world has bounds and limits to what can be known, fairy tales seek to open another field of experience through the unrestrained action of the imagination:

The fairy tale world is the "long, long ago" world of infinite possibility, existing now only in and through the imagination. Entering into the realm of possibility is dangerous—for possibility includes both vision and nightmare—but necessary for wholeness. The risk of the imagination is most assuredly a temptation, the risk of chaos for the possibility of knowledge which is truth, truth which is beauty. ("Christina Rossetti," 70)

In the logic of fairy tales, the moral tale is too timid to win heaven; the moral tale's rejection of the imagination is challenged absolutely by the fairy tale's embrace of the fantastic sublime. Patient faith and waiting for salvation are thrown over for an immediate attempt to realize the world of the spirit through the imagination, in this case, the fairy fruit of the imagination unbound. In *Goblin Market*, the apparent moral tale is overthrown for the courage to seek for the fruit now.

As the critic Janet Casey writes of the roles played by Laura and

Lizzie and of the two competing readings of the poem:

At first glance their roles seem obvious: Lizzie is the redeemer and Laura the redeemed. Just as Laura is the fallen Eve figure, Lizzie becomes a Christ figure, scourged by the goblins and ultimately presenting herself to Laura as a kind of Eucharist: "Eat me, drink me, love me." In a very subtle manner, however, Rossetti allows Lizzie to play the part of the redeemed as well as the redeemer. As we have already seen, Lizzie lacks the courage of action that is Laura's. Laura's fall sets in motion the chain of events which forces Lizzie to gain that courage. (68)

Casey points to one passage that contains "even a subtle suggestion that the timid Lizzie recognizes her need to acquire some of Laura's courage" (68):

Tender Lizzie could not bear
To watch her sister's cankerous care
Yet not to share. (31)

Envy does underlie the wording here, a wordplay reminiscent of the earlier phrase "locked in one nest," which images Laura and Lizzie clasped together but also locked away, as prisoners, from the world of the fairy fruit and its gift of the sublime moment. Lizzie becomes not a simple Christ figure, but another redeemer closer to the heart of the Romantics, Prometheus, the fire stealer who contends for the divine: Laura's withering is like the trial of Prometheus bound to the rocks, the price he had to pay for stealing fire; Laura in her joy is "like a leaping flame" (23), the stolen gift of Prometheus, and fire imagery becomes ever more frequent in Lizzie's tale, a recurring metaphor for the consuming joy of the sublime that Lizzie will win.

Lizzie, spurred by Laura's pain and her example, gains the fairy fruit by moving beyond her notions of "her place" and what "should be," beyond the division of home and "haunted glen," beyond the split of the masculine and feminine:

till Laura dwindling
Seemed knocking at Death's door:
Then Lizzie weighed no more
Better and worse. (32)

Instead, leaving behind division, "Better and worse," she opens her eyes on the world of the spirit, and so to the promise and risk of "joy beyond the walls of the world poignant as grief." Lizzie,

> At twilight, halted by the brook:
> And for the first time in her life
> Began to listen and look. (33)

The goblins act, at first, as they acted with Laura; they come for her in a bewildering array of forms half-glimpsed, speaking in incomprehensible animal voices and offering their impossible fruits.

> Laughed every goblin
> When he spied her peeping:
> Came toward her hobbling,
> Flying, running, leaping,
> Puffing and blowing,
> Chuckling, clapping, crowing,
> Clucking and gobbling,
> Mopping and mowing,
> Full of airs and graces,
> Pulling wry faces,
> Demure grimaces,
> Cat-like and rat-like,
> Ratel- and wombat-like,
> Snail-paced in a hurry,
> Parrot-voiced and whistler,
> Helter skelter, hurry skurry,
> Chattering like magpies,
> Fluttering like pigeons,
> Gliding like fishes,—
> Hugged and kissed her;
> Squeezed and caressed her;
> Stretched up their dishes,
> Panniers, and plates:
> "Look at our apples
> Russet and dun,
> Bob at our cherries,
> Bite at our peaches,
> Citrons and dates,
> Grapes for the asking,

Pears red with basking
Out in the sun,
Plums on their twigs;
Pluck them and suck them,
Pomegranates, figs." (33-5)

The sing-song rhymes used to describe the sinister and seductive goblin men highlights the unreadability of the goblins; their strange language—blowing, chuckling, crowing, clucking, gobbling, chattering like magpies—their odd movements—fluttering like pigeons, gliding like fishes—and their inappropriate actions—hugged and kissed her, squeezed and caressed her—all make one squirm without being able to say what exactly is wrong; just that nothing is right.

The goblin men become, if anything, more overwhelming, more frightening, than during Laura's encounter with them. Perhaps Lizzie, who is aware of the risk she takes—is "Mindful of Jeanie" (35)—and knows the goblins mean her no good will, simply sees the goblins more clearly than Laura did. Lizzie asks for fruit to carry away and will not eat. She offers a silver penny, not waiting for the goblin men to set their price, countering their desire to take her hair or her tears with the offer from the real world, an offer of a decidedly nonfairy currency, money. The goblin men insist she must eat the fruits immediately, or their potency would fade, must eat them there with the goblin men, or nothing would come of it:

Such fruits as these
No man can carry;
Half their bloom would fly,
Half their dew would dry,
Half their flavour would pass by. (38)

Lizzie will not relent and the goblins are confounded and become angry:

They began scratching their pates,
No longer wagging, purring,
But visibly demurring,
Grunting and snarling.
One called her proud,

Cross-grained, uncivil;
Their tones waxed loud,
Their looks were evil.
Lashing their tails
They trod and hustled her,
Elbowed and jostled her,
Clawed with their nails,
Barking, mewing, hissing, mocking,
Tore her gown and soiled her stocking,
Twitched her hair out by the roots,
Stamped upon her tender feet,
Held her hands and squeezed their fruits
Against her mouth to make her eat. (39-40)

Lizzie endures a symbolic rape, as well as physical abuse. The goblin men attempt to take what will not be given to them, power.

The critic Dolores Rosenblum identifies Lizzie's endurance as particularly feminine:

this is typical female strength, the strength of a mother, for instance, who will not only fight like a tiger but also, when the circumstances demand it, use guile and endure humiliation to save her child. Lizzie's heroic fortitude transforms the eroticized similes that have been used to illustrate Laura's downfall into images of resplendent female power. (79)

Rosenblum also notes that Lizzie's watching over Laura when she lay ill was a typical female act of redemption (82), and writes:

Goblin Market represents a rediscovery of true female origins and a rejection of the patriarchal quest myth, or, rather, a reappropriation of it as a female myth. (83)

While Laura's tale reveals the failure of the fantastic sublime, *Goblin Market* is, finally, an appropriation and not a rejection of the sublime. Lizzie attempts to get what the goblin men are hoarding, revealing the goblin men to be not simply evil-doers, although they are certainly wicked to Laura, but, in a sense, competitors, fellow seekers of the sublime. As the critic Jeanie Watson writes, the goblin merchant men, "who presumably also eat the fruit they sell" ("Christina Rossetti," 71), are akin to the ecstatic poet of Coleridge's "Kubla

Khan," against whom "all should cry, Beware! Beware!" (49-50) and then "close your eyes with holy dread,/ For he on honeydew has fed,/ And drunk the milk of Paradise" (lines 52-4). The rich and impossible fairy fruit hold the promise of both "honey" and "poison," of honeydew and the milk of Paradise, and holy dread. The goblin men are spiritual seekers lost themselves in the world of the spirit, perhaps forced to haunt the glen by desire for the women and the lost world of community and family. Ultimately, they are akin as well to the Ancient Mariner from Coleridge's "Rime of the Ancient Mariner," seemingly compelled to their cry and to wander in the night; certainly they leave Laura, as the Mariner left the Wedding Guest, sadder if not wiser.

Lizzie does not reject the fruit of the goblin men, only the terms the goblins set. She changes the rules and will not give in:

> Though the goblins cuffed and caught her,
> Coaxed and fought her,
> Bullied and besought her,
> Scratched her, pinched her black as ink,
> Kicked and knocked her,
> Mauled and mocked her,
> Lizzie uttered not a word;
> Would not open lip from lip
> Lest they cram a mouthful in. (44)

This key moment in *Goblin Market* when the juice is smeared on Lizzie's body, is, curiously, the crux of both the Christian allegorical, that is, the moral tale, and the fairy tale readings of the poem.

The closed mouth, which would not utter "a word," is the moment of Lizzie's Christ-like redemption of Laura, a redemption seemingly built on the renunciation of the fairy fruit, the "forbidden" fruit of Eden, and so of original sin. But Lizzie, in the fairy tale of the "positive" sublime, is not Christ but Prometheus; in this moment she steals the "fiery" fruit of the imagination as Prometheus stole fire itself. Her closed mouth is part of a compromise sublime—an alternative to what the goblins insist is the only way, the male way, to get the fairy fruit. Instead of running, like Bunyan's Christian, into the world of the spirit, toward death and renunciation of this world, leaving family and love behind, she heals the split between worlds, bringing back to the world of hearth and home not the dead kernel Laura brought but the juice of the spirit fruit itself, the transcendent joy, "honey to the throat," without the "poison" sting. Lizzie discovers not an absolute sublime such as Diamond achieved—a journey into death and the world of the spirit, complete and utter—but a feminine sublime as suggested by Mellor's reading of Mary Shelley's *Frankenstein*, a domesticated sublimity. As Rosenblum writes:

Laura, of course, is intent on finding out and getting things for herself, like a folk or epic hero. But her quest and her calamity demystify the heroic thrust toward self-definition. There is another way, Rossetti seems to be saying: there are situations in which standing firm and being for another are more integrative and potent than going forth and being for oneself. What the sisters acquire and demonstrate by the end of the poem is a particularly female—but not necessarily renunciatory—wisdom. (71)

Laura's tale opened the promise of the goblin men and found it empty. Lizzie's tale actively shows another way to get inside the fairy fruit to the sweet sap; by not eating but receiving the syrup of the fruit for another, in an act built on foreknowledge, resistance and compassion for another, Lizzie overwhelms the goblins:

Lizzie's act is no mean or cowardly act of submission, but one of defiance and action; it is a decisive act of will, and in the face of strength the goblin men slink and slime their way back into the primal depths of their origin. (Shurbutt, 42)

The goblins indeed melt—writhe away, disappear, vanish in the distance—like the Wicked Witch of the West in L. Frank Baum's *The Wizard of Oz* (1900). Rossetti's poem and the famous 1939 movie adaption starring Judy Garland (but not the original story) of Baum's work even contain parallel acts done for another which banish wickedness. As Dorothy's attempt to put out the fire on the Scarecrow both saves Scarecrow and melts the Witch, Lizzie's act for another both saves Laura and expels the goblins. The goblins,

Worn out by her resistance,
Flung back her penny, kicked their fruit,
Along whichever road they took,

Not leaving root or stone or shoot;
Some writhed in the ground,
Some dived into the brook
With ring and ripple,
Some scudded on the gale without a sound,
Some vanished in the distance.   (44-45)

The goblins become irrelevant as Lizzie relocates the sublime from the "haunted glen" into her home where Laura wastes away. She tempers the transcendence of the sublime with both personal will and the ties of human, as well as divine, love, actively preventing the sublime experience from ending in blockage. Lizzie experiences joy even as the goblins maul her: she "laughed in heart to feel the drip/ Of juice that syrupped her face" (44). Her fear gives way to gaiety: she is no longer "pricked by fear" but instead feels "inward laughter" (46). Just like Laura before her, she "Knew not was it night or day" (45).

Lizzie, by domesticating the sublime, manufactures the transcendence of the third phase of Weiskel's structure of the sublime through an act of selflessness that replaces the (male) fantastic sublime's more forceful self-forgetfulness or loosening of the self in the transcendent experience of the world of the spirit. The absolute transcendence of Diamond, Christian or, for that matter, Laura, is forsaken in a move that again seems to follow the renunciation of sin in Christian life, but that is also a cultivation of the joy of the sublime, a harvesting that brings that joy home, a move that has little or nothing to do with renunciation.

An inclusive reading will demonstrate what is evident from the sensuousness, luxuriance, cheerfulness, and energy of the poem and from the serenity of the ending: that it is not a poem of bitter repression but rather a fantasy of feminine freedom, heroism, and self-sufficiency and a celebration of sisterly and maternal love. (Mermin, 108)

More than that, *Goblin Market* is a fantasy of the sublime achieved. As the scene of Lizzie's homecoming demonstrates, the erotic love, which belonged exclusively to the goblin men of the haunted glen at the beginning of the poem, is bought home. Lizzie calls to Laura, offering herself as, indeed, a "kind of Eucharist," a spirit in the flesh that intimates the eater into the mystery of the divine:

Did you miss me?
Come and kiss me.
Never mind my bruises,
Hug me, kiss me, suck my juices
Squeezed from goblin fruits for you,
Goblin pulp and goblin dew.
Eat me, drink me, love me;
Laura make much of me;
For your sake I have braved the glen
And had to do with goblin merchant men. (46-7)

Joyful fire, the image in the poem of the soul transcendent, also moves from the tasting of the fruit in the haunted glen of goblin men into the sisters' safe home. When Lizzie held out against the goblins' anger, she is "Like a beacon left alone/ In a hoary roaring sea,/ sending up a golden fire" (40). Fire out of water is an image of opposites melded into one, of the worlds of spirit and home together, masculine and feminine. As Laura "kissed and kissed her [Lizzie] with a hungry mouth./ Her lips began to scorch" (48) and "like a caged thing freed" she revived, a leaping flame, from her slow withering:

Swift fire spread through her veins, knocked at her heart,
Met the fire smoldering there
And overbore its lesser flame. (49)

The images of "fire" and "lesser flame" identify the joy Lizzie brings home as the same joy Laura briefly attained from the goblin men, but with its promise sustained. The domesticated fantastic sublime is also experienced as joyful fire, the core of the sublime experience remaining the same.

As *Goblin Market* reaches its frame and end, becoming a tale retold by the two sisters, now older, to their children, it becomes more clearly both a warning and a guide for getting the fairy fruit:

Laura turns the encounter with the goblins into a tale told and retold as a ritual to bind the children together, and the moral she draws from it is not that girls should avoid goblins—the sisters seem to remember them, in fact, with some pleasure—but that "there is no friend like a sister." (Mermin, 117)

The sisters describe their experience with the goblin men to their children as:

> Those pleasant days long gone
> Of not returning time:
> Would talk about the haunted glen,
> The wicked, quaint fruit-merchant men,
> Their fruits like honey in the throat
> But poison to the blood. (52)

The "wicked" and "poison" of the last half of this quote become almost playful under the influence of "pleasant" at the opening. If the tale had not been told, and Laura's fate not been witnessed by the reader as dire, one might suspect them of hyperbole in their warnings.

The final moral begs discussion, particularly because it appears to bound the Christian allegorical reading of the poem:

> For there is no friend like a sister
> In calm or stormy weather;
> To cheer one on the tedious way,
> To fetch one if one goes astray,
> To lift one if one totters down,
> To strengthen whilst one stands. (53)

The imagery seems to support Lizzie's Christ-like redemption of Laura who has "gone astray." However, the moral repeats the controlling trope of the poem, the equality of sisterhood that does not privilege one sister and disparage the other. Moreover, the moral seems wholly inadequate to the story of the sublime, especially in its sexual dimension, brought home into the sisters' world.

The inadequacy of the moral is reminiscent of Coleridge's "Rime of the Ancient Mariner," where the moral hardly bounds the terrifying and fantastic incidents preceding it:

> He prayeth best, who loveth best
> All things both great and small;
> For the dear God who loveth us,
> He made and loveth all. (614-7)

Coleridge's "Rime," like *Goblin Market*, has two competing readings, one a moral tale of natural piety, the other a fairy tale of invisible spirits. Again, the final moral bounds and seems to affirm the moral tale, except, as with Rossetti's work, it just is not up to the task. The homilies of Coleridge's moral do not do justice to the awful spirit nine fathoms deep and the supernatural power that holds the Mariner in thrall long after he blesses the seasnakes unaware, long after, that is, he supposedly experiences grace and redemption.

The comments Coleridge and Rossetti made about the meaning of their tales are significant. Coleridge, after the poet Mrs. Barbauld complained that his "Rime" lacked a moral (a comment which, as the moral hardly contains the poem, is apt), responded:

the only, or chief fault, if I might say so, was the obtrusion of the moral sentiment so openly on the reader as a principle or cause of action in a work of such pure imagination. It ought to have had no more moral than the Arabian Nights' tale of the merchant's sitting down to eat dates by the side of a well, and throwing the shells aside, and lo! a genie starts up, and says he *must* kill the aforesaid merchant *because* one of the date shells had, it seems, put out the eye of the genie's son. (*Table Talk*, 86, 31 May, 1830)

William Michael Rossetti, Christina's brother, writes that he "more than once heard Christina say that she did not mean anything profound by this fairy tale" (459). The morals, the proposed meaning of the works, are tossed aside by the authors who acknowledge that they fail to express the meaning of their tales of "pure imagination." These comments are curious, since the final morals exist, and transform the appended morals in each work from actual summation into what is acknowledged as inadequate attempts at closure, attempts that only underscore how frightening and uncontrollable the imagination unbound really is in each work; the morals express the desperate *need* for closure by the sisters and the poor Mariner as opposed to actually providing it.

In *Goblin Market*, the end of the tale can be found not in the moral but in the retelling of the tale itself:

The children listen—as do we—fascinated and intrigued by the story of the goblin men and their fruit. And Christina Rossetti, by letting her female character tell a fairy tale which delights and entertains as the children join "hands to little hands" to form a magic circle, affirms the truth of the imagination and knowledge over conventional moral conduct. Maidens have the right to buy the fruit of Goblin Market. (Watson, "Christina Rossetti," 75)

The truth of fairy tales, of fantasy, impossible to summarize, exists only in the irreducible images themselves. Such images, although described in words, suggest something beyond language's ability to explain or encompass. Rossetti's work presents its unstatable "fairy" moral simply by repeating—passing down from mother to daughter—the fairy story of how women might look on the imagination unbound and not end up like Jeanie.

Chapter 12

Difference and Common Ground

Nineteenth-century children's fantasy literature contains a split between a celebrated male tradition—including works widely read even today—and a larger but now obscure countertradition of female writers, mostly writing moral tales, but, as the century wore on, increasingly employing fairy tale material. From the beginning of the nineteenth century to its end, women wrote most children's literature, but, as the critics Auerbach and Knoepflmacher observe in their book, *Forbidden Journeys*:

the most acclaimed writers of Victorian children's fantasies were three eccentric men—Lewis Carroll, George MacDonald, and James Barrie—whose obsessive nostalgia for their own idealized childhoods inspired them to imagine dream countries where no one had to grow up. The most moving Victorian children's books are steeped in longing for unreachable lives. Carroll, MacDonald, and Barrie envied the children they could not be; out of this envious longing came their painful children's classics.

Most Victorian women . . . envied adults rather than children. Whether they were wives and mothers or teachers and governesses, respectable women's lives had as their primary object child care. British law made the link between women and children indelible by denying women independent legal representation. . . . In theory, at any rate, women lived the condition Carroll, MacDonald, and Barrie longed for. If they were good, they never grew up. (1)

Lewis Carroll's Alice, James Barrie's Peter Pan, and George MacDonald's Diamond are fantasies of an eternal childhood where Alice "leaves off at seven," Peter does not age and Diamond dies happy and young.

In the nineteenth century, especially in children's fantasy literature by women, the fairy tale and the moral tale move towards one another. As seen in the first chapter of this work, fairy tales, largely banned at the end of the eighteenth century, had been transformed in the early part of the nineteenth century from adult works—full with adult measures of sex and violence—into tales meant for the imaginative Romantic child, thereby easing into the mainstream of society. Moral tales, the dominant children's literature of the eighteenth century, increasingly employed fairy tale material in the second half of the nineteenth century in imitation of the runaway success of fantasy fiction, but often in such a dry and didactic way as to drain any magic out in the service of moral instruction, a heavy-handedness that led to the moral tale's fading out altogether by the early twentieth century.

The success of the largely male tradition of fantasy over the largely female tradition of the moral tale is ironic, since the original fairy tale tradition, the banned tradition of the eighteenth century and earlier (no one can say how much earlier), had been appropriated, more or less, from women by men, starting with the Brothers Grimm and reaching its apotheosis, perhaps, in Lewis Carroll's fantasy of the little girl who must never grow up. The fairy tale tradition before the nineteenth century had been an oral narrative tradition, and though male storytellers must have told the tales along with female storytellers, the prominence of figures like "Mother Goose" show how strongly the fairy tales were identified with women. As Auerbach and Knoepflmacher speculate, the anonymity and indeterminate antiquity of the fairy tale tradition point to it as possibly a "lost, distinctively female tradition" (3). The nineteenth-century scholars and collectors of fairy tales, as well as the most celebrated innovators of nineteenth-century literary fairy tales, were almost exclusively men.

Female fantasists who wrote children's fairy tales—fantasists like Rossetti whose moral tale is overwhelmed by fairy in *Goblin Market*—found themselves working in a genre distinctly gendered, and requiring reinterpretation to include, reinclude, women. As Auerbach and Knoepflmacher write, the anger expressed by Victorian female fantasists is directed not only at all the forms of authority and convention satirized and confounded by the children's fantasy literature of the male writers, but "also undermines the ideological assumptions and literary conventions of those privileged men" (6), the nineteenth-century male fantasists themselves. The men, for better or worse, perhaps better *and* worse, are the tradition in the nineteenth century. Women fantasists found themselves having to appropriate, or rather, reappropriate, the genre before telling their tales, which, however, after the wild fantasies of male writers like Edward Lear in his *Book of Nonsense* (1846) and Lewis Carroll in *Alice in Wonderland* (1865) allowed a freedom of form and expression unavailable before mid-century.

The relationship between the nineteenth-century male and female writers of children's fantasy literature was, for the women at least, a disturbing paradox; they owed a literary debt to the male fantasists but also seemed to experience the works by the men to be a problem, a burden. As Auerbach and Knoepflmacher explain of the influence of Carroll's *Alice in Wonderland*:

> If, on the one hand, the success of the *Alice* books had licensed female dreaming and liberated aggressive subtexts for women writers, Carroll's nostalgia, his resistance to female growth and female sexuality, could hardly inspire Ewing, Ingelow, and Rossetti as they transported their own child heroines into realms of the forbidden. As they recognized, the frustration of Carroll's intense desire to keep his beloved dream child forever young, forever enshrined in "happy summer days" unaffected by change, led him to indulge in fantasies of containment and domination that were totally inimical to their own yearning for autonomy and authority. Although the author of the *Alice* books may impersonate ineffectual male creatures such as the White Rabbit and the White Knight, he is also angry at the girl who refuses to "leave off at seven" and prefers, instead, to grow into an adult woman. (6)

Jean Ingelow (1820-1897) is best remembered for *Mopsa the Fairy* (1869). Juliana Ewing (1841-1885) wrote short stories for children, which appeared often in the Victorian periodical *Aunt Judy's Magazine*. A brief examination of works by each author can serve to illustrate common motifs in nineteenth-century children's fantasy literature by women in comparison with works by men.

While imaginative children are revered in children's fantasy in general, their absolute purity is dethroned in works by women. Rather, drawing on the wisdom of the moral tale, and perhaps on the evidence available from their greater role in child rearing, children in fantasy literature by women are more often willful and in need of correction. Fairyland often turns out to be, although often still a glimpse of the world of spirit, a purgatory. In Ewing's "Amelia and the Dwarfs," the title character, a rude little girl, when taken into fairyland, is made to wash all the frocks she dirtied, mend all the "gimcracks" she has broken, and pick up "the broken threads of all the conversations you have interrupted" (122). This kind of correction and instruction is not as much fun as the pure nonsense of a writer like Edward Lear and accounts for much of the obscurity of many nineteenth-century children's works by women.

However, as a corollary, nineteenth-century children's fantasy by women is more often concerned with growth and responsibility than are works by men. At the end of Ingelow's *Mopsa the Fairy*, Mopsa becomes a Fairy Queen, finding her rightful place and banishing her friend (and the apparent protagonist of the novel early on) Jack. In the end, Jack forgets all about Mopsa, but she admits pain and memory into her life, achieving a maturity Jack has yet to imagine. The growth of Mopsa and the lack of growth of Jack makes a scathing commentary on the static children of much nineteenth-century children's literature by men. The precious eternal children of fantasy literature never experience the suffering and complex joy of adulthood. The divisions described are far from absolute, the impulse for growth from the moral tale and joy from the fairy tale eventually fusing in children's literature toward the end of the nineteenth century, but the comparison does fairly characterize the two styles of writing.

The division between growth and stasis holds up, at least at first glance, in comparisons of Rossetti's work to Grahame's and MacDonald's. Where Toad is not an altered Toad at the end of *The Wind in the Willows*, and Diamond in *At the Back of the North Wind* achieves perfection and eternal childhood only through death, Rossetti's *Goblin Market*, in contrast, ends with growth and aging; Laura and Lizzie begin as maidens and end as mothers. The passing down to their children of the tale of the goblin men is itself an act of shared community between generations, steeped in the passage of time, accepting it uncritically. As the critic Dolores Rosenblum writes:

Like other myths and fairy tales, *Goblin Market* is also about the fall from innocence into experience, a "natural" process which leads to the "unnatural" and purely human growth into self-consciousness and freely chosen participation in communal life. (71)

At second glance, one might notice that communal life also informs Kenneth Grahame's pastoral fantasy *The Wind in the Willows*, and that Mole, unlike, Toad, does learn and change, as both a Romantic seeker of the sublime and a lover of home and comfort. The similarities between Rossetti's work and Grahame's even suggest that the intense gender arguments locked in much nineteenth-century children's fantasies are not inherent to the sublime or the fantastic, reflecting instead nineteenth-century social and political reality. Kenneth Grahame's bachelor brotherhood of Mole, Rat, Toad and Badger matches Rossetti's sisterhood of Laura and Lizzie. Considering the Romantic seekers in Grahame's work are just Mole and Rat, the comparison may really be between two seekers and two seekers. Much more importantly, the balance between transcendence and home, "that anchor in one's existence," is of central importance in both works. Both works champion the realization of the sublime, balanced by a life of comfort and happiness.

Grahame's work, in retrospect, offers a kind of domesticated sublimity much like Rossetti's work. Grahame, in his chapter on the Sea Rat, "Wayfarers All," recognizes the dangers of the sublime, and in "Dulce Domum" emphasizes the need for "some place to come back to" in the midst of the pursuit of the fantastic sublime. Rossetti's work, of course, is fraught with the danger of the sublime, a danger overcome finally only by the strength of community and home. Each writer is concerned with not losing touch with either the world of comfort and friendship or the world of transcendent joy and sublime experience; how to achieve both provides the central impetus to the tales of Laura and Lizzie and Rat and Mole.

However, each work is still distinctly gendered: as Rossetti's work is curiously absent of (human) men as husbands, Grahame's is curiously absent of (animal) women as wives. The experience of the fantastic sublime in Rossetti's work is hard won; the sisters essentially steal the sublime and bring it back home. In Grahame's work, the fantastic sublime of Pan requires the typical movement of the male Romantic seekers outward into spirit, into a world close by, relatively easy to obtain and free from noxious after-effects.

Kenneth Grahame relocated the Romantic experience of nature into the imagination only gently, striking a careful balance between the spirit and the physical, largely recapitulating the Romantic sublime faithfully. Yet his fantasy, if less radically than MacDonald's, was centered in childhood. The critic Sheila Egoff remarked of *The Wind in the Willows*: "Its true genesis lies in the two semi-autobiographical accounts of Grahame's childhood. . . . *The Golden Age* (1895) and *Dream Days* (1898)" (100). In those works, the adults are known as The Olympians, remote, powerful and enigmatic. The narrator writes of them:

Indeed, it was one of the most hopeless features in their character (when we troubled ourselves to waste a thought on them: which wasn't often) that, having license to indulge in the pleasures of life, they could get no good of it. They might dabble in the pond all day, hunt the chickens, climb trees in the most uncompromising Sunday clothes; . . .yet they never did any one of these things. (*The Golden Age*, 190)

Egoff remarks:

The Golden Age, *Dream Days* and *The Wind in the Willows* are not linked through animal lore; animals are hardly mentioned in the first two books. However, these books all have a feeling of a private separate world. (101)

The children lived separate from The Olympians, just as the world of *The Wind in the Willows* is cut off from the Wide World. In the contained world of the Riverbank, Grahame found a metaphor for eternal childhood; the children of *The Golden Age* and *Dream Days* must grow up, but the riverbankers, who are already adults, but of a different order, must only keep the Wide World at bay. The "poop-poop" of Toad's motor cars, however, sounds a warning of the fragility of Grahame's imagined haven.

Kenneth Grahame yearns for an eternal world without the strain of growing up much as did Carroll, Barrie and MacDonald. His adults are adults without work or family, without the responsibilities of adulthood, while Rossetti's world of home embraces chores and caring for children as part and parcel of the experience of home. Mole never does complete his whitewashing. Grahame's world of the riverbankers occupies some kind of an intermediate space—fragile and rare—balanced between the Wide World and the transcendent sublime. The world of the riverbankers must remain hidden from the Wide World, the world of what Grahame calls, in an essay from his collection *The Pagan Papers*, "unblest hurry" ("The Romance of the Road," 17). In essay after essay, Grahame longs for "days outside history . . . when kindly beasts would loiter to give counsel by the wayside" ("The Fairy Wicket," 157). The presiding spirit of those lost days outside history is a frail, beleaguered spirit, Pan, a beauty existing only when remaining out of sight: "Out of hearing of all the clamor, the rural Pan may be found . . . by the secluded stream of the sinuous Mole, abounding in friendly greetings for his foster-brothers the dab-chick and water-rat" ("The Rural Pan," 68).

These desires are a desire for a world beside the world, a world where Faerie lies close at hand, a world Grahame describes as all margin, the forgotten text beside the text, lying between the text itself and the emptiness beyond all text. In "Deus Terminus," he describes the margin as the imagination unknown and unbound:

It is only the old enchantment that is gone; banished by the matter-of-fact deity, who has stolidly settled exactly where Lord A.'s shooting ends and Squire B.'s begins. Once, no such petty limitations fettered the mind. A step into the woodland was a step over the border—the margin of the material. (96)

In an essay on "Marginalia," Grahame wonders:

when shall the true poet arise who, disdaining the trivialities of text, shall give the world a book of verse consisting entirely of margin? How we shall shove and jostle for large paper copies! (81)

In yet another essay, Grahame relates his fantasy of a stockbroker who leaves his work suddenly to walk in the green fields instead of working in his "wonted corner." He is put back in his place, "And yet—let the sun shine too wantonly in Throgmorton street, let an errant zephyr, quick with the warm south, fan but his cheek too wooingly on his way to the station; and will he not once more snap his chain and away?" (189, "Orion"). This call of the wind describes exactly what did happen to Mole while whitewashing. While Rossetti closes the magic circle of the home in the clasped hands of the children at the end of *Goblin Market*, Grahame sought the sublime beyond the home, despite the importance of home in his work.

MacDonald also, and more clearly, sought the sublime in Grahame's "margin of the material." But for MacDonald the margin, far from being frail or hidden, was the true world beyond, behind, between and above the world, greater and larger, apprehended through the imagination. Describing the imagination, MacDonald writes: "It is, therefore, that faculty in man likest to the prime operation of the power of God. . . ." ("The Imagination," 2). The imagination of man is comprehended in the imagination of God. It contains truth, and the world around us is but a shadow of its light:

The imagination of man is made in the image of the imagination of God. Everything of man must have been of God first; and it will help much towards our understanding of the imagination and its functions in man if we first succeeded in regarding aright the imagination of God, in which the imagination of man lives and moves and has its being. ("The Imagination," 3)

Or, more succinctly: "Man is but a thought of God" ("The Imagination," 4).

MacDonald describes the relationship of the known, bound world and the unknown in a striking image:

our consciousness is to the extent of our being but as the flame of the volcano to the world-gulf whence it issues: in the gulf of our unknown being God works behind our consciousness. (*Unspoken Sermons*, 2:113)

Grahame's hidden riverbank pales beside that world-gulf, and its lava light outshines Rossetti's stolen fire. On the strength of MacDonald's faith, the world becomes nearly obliterated by the light shining through it. Striving to enter the other world becomes the only true act and the only way home.

MacDonald's notion of the imagination draws from Coleridge's formulation of the primary imagination in the *Biographia Literaria*:

The primary IMAGINATION I hold to be the living power and prime agent of all human perception, and as a repetition in the finite mind of the eternal act of creation in the infinite I AM. (1:304)

The world, for MacDonald, is finite, while the imagination can, through fantasy, take part in the infinite of God beyond the world. MacDonald also uses Coleridge's distinction between the imagination and fancy, writing of humanity:

there is that in him which delights in calling up new forms—which is the nearest he can come to creation. When such forms are new embodiments of old truths, we call them products of the Imagination; when they are mere inventions, however lovely, I should call them the work of the Fancy. ("Fantastic Imagination," 314)

As he writes elsewhere, "better to keep the word creation for that calling out of nothing which is the imagination of God" ("The Imagination," 3). Fantasy that does not suggest anything beyond itself is "mere invention"; only the fantasy of the fantastic sublime, which attempts to move beyond the words themselves to somehow apprehend the infinite I AM beyond, is truth. For Coleridge, the infinite I AM is the eternal glimpsed by the finite mind, the world of the spirit, the consubstantial world, experienced through the imagination.

Rossetti's *Goblin Market*, Grahame's *The Wind in the Willows* and MacDonald's *At the Back of the North Wind* are all bound together as works of the imagination and the fantastic sublime. Despite differences, they are nevertheless part of one tradition, not simply as fantasy, or even nineteenth century children's fantasy, but as part of a peculiar group of works interested in transcendence through what MacDonald calls "the fantastic imagination." They affirm a spiritual dimension to fantasy and explore, through fantastic images, the meaning and experience of spirit.

After all, the dangers as well as the pleasures of the sublime underwrote the poetry of Wordsworth and Coleridge as much as it did Rossetti's work. Grahame's work even contains attempts to realize the sublime parallel to those of Laura and Lizzie; Mole's failure in the Wild

Wood is followed by his success on Pan's island. Rossetti's stark gendering of the blockage of the sublime is also perhaps little more than a move to reverse what the (male) nineteenth-century collectors of fairy tales did to fantasy in their selection, editing and revising of fairy tales. Perhaps, in the end, the difference between male and female nineteenth-century children's fantasy literature, while important to note, only reveals them to be but mirror images of one another, essentially bound together by a longing for the transcendence revealed in their shared genre of the fantastic.

Many other forms of fantasy exist, of course, with as many different aims or purposes. Gothic literature, much discussed in this work, initially similar in structure to the fantastic sublime, up to the moment of transcendence, ends only in blockage, collapse and overwhelming anxiety or fear. Another kind of fantasy works self-consciously at word play and word games as a means of subverting and discovering the limits of language, and thereby the limits of consciousness. Language, never able to reach beyond to some notion of the transcendent, is the limit never escaped, yet all its certainties are undermined and its limits in question. This form is more modern, a part of much "literary" fantasy and American (but not necessarily Latin American) forms of "magic realism." Lewis Carroll's *Alice in Wonderland* plays between genres, including rhetorical fantasy and, as discussed elsewhere in this book, the fantastic sublime; its ability to be read as a rhetorical fantasy has had as much to do with its critical acclaim in our time as its joyous fun and strange occurrences. Fantasy as pure rhetoric is considered more sophisticated, in an unreligious age, than a kind of fantasy that continues to search for a new way to approach the world of the spirit as old ways fall aside.

Since the fantastic sublime cannot, of course, prove the existence of anything beyond itself—looked for, the world of the spirit cannot be found in the texts themselves—and guarantees transcendence only through the participation of the imagination of the reader as well as of the author, even works of the sublime can be read as purely rhetorical. This approach has been successful in studying Romanticism as well. The moment of transcendence can be successfully read as the breakdown of language and meaning, the limit of the mind's ability to regard itself. This work, however, has been interested in taking at face value—that is, in the emotional terms used to describe it—the experience of the imagination in achieving transcendence in a small but coherent tradition of a kind of fantasy literature.

C.S. Lewis admired George MacDonald who admired William Wordsworth. C.S. Lewis and J.R.R. Tolkien joined in the same writing group, The Inklings. Lewis Carroll read the unpublished manuscript for *Alice in Wonderland* to George MacDonald's children. Lewis Carroll and George MacDonald were ordained ministers as well as writers. Lewis, Tolkien, MacDonald and Rossetti wrote often of their Christian beliefs and applied their beliefs to their works, both in fantasy and elsewhere. This work has been interested in shared ideas, the evolution of those ideas and how the authors both *said* they would apply those ideas and how those ideas worked themselves out in their fantastic stories. Specifically, this work concerned itself with the appropriation and reinterpretation of the Romantic notion of the sublime by nineteenth-century fantasists, and their creation of the fantastic sublime, an act that sought to define and refine fantastic literature and has implications for every genre of the fantastic, from the Gothic to science fiction. The reader and critic must decide for themselves, however, whether what was found was "an insignificant thing that can neither flash nor fly," as MacDonald wrote, or truth. Both, if MacDonald's parable of the firefly that "now flashes, now is dark" can be believed, are present, dependent on faith.

Bibliography

Abrams, M.H. "The Correspondent Breeze: A Romantic Metaphor." *The Correspondent Breeze: Essays on English Romanticism.* New York: Norton, 1984. 25-43.

Alexander, Lloyd. "Wishful Thinking—or Hopeful Dreaming?" *The Horn Book Magazine.* August, 1968: 383-90. Rpt. in *Fantasists on Fantasy: A Collection of Critical Reflections By Eighteen Masters of the Art.* Eds. Robert H. Boyer and Kenneth J. Zahorski. New York: Avon, 1984. 140-9.

Aries, Phillipe. *Centuries of Childhood: A Social History of Family Life.* Trans. Robert Baldick. 1962. New York: Knopf, 1970.

Arseneau, Mary. "Incarnation and Interpretation: Christina Rossetti, the Oxford Movement, and *Goblin Market.*" *Victorian Poetry.* 31:3 (Spring, 1993): 79-93.

Auerbach, Nina and U.C. Knoepflmacher, Eds. "Introduction." *Forbidden Journeys, Fairy Tales and Fantasies by Victorian Women Writers.* Chicago: University of Chicago Press, 1992. 1-10.

Bettelheim, Bruno. *The Uses of Enchantment: The Meaning and Importance of Fairy Tales.* New York: Knopf, 1976.

Blake, William. "Introduction." *The Songs of Innocence and Experience.* 1789. 1789 ed. New York: Orion, 1967.

Bloom, Harold. "Frankenstein, or the Modern Prometheus." *The Ringers in the Tower: Studies in Romantic Tradition.* Chicago: University of Chicago Press, 1971. 119-29.

———. "Freud and the Poetic Sublime: A Catastrophe Theory of Creativity" (1978) in *Freud: A Collection of Critical Essays.* Ed. Perry Meisel. Englewood, NJ: Prentice, 1981.

Bottigheimer, Ruth B. *Grimms' Bad Girls and Bold Boys: The Moral and*

Social Vision of the Tales. New Haven: Yale University Press, 1987.

Browne, Francis. *Granny's Wonderful Chair.* 1856. New York: Puffin, 1985.

Calvino, Italo. *Italian Folktales.* Trans. George Martin. New York: Pantheon, 1980.

Carpenter, Humphrey. *Secret Gardens: A Study of the Golden Age of Children's Literature.* Boston: Houghton, 1985.

Carroll, Lewis. *The Annotated Alice: Alice's Adventures in Wonderland & Through the Looking Glass.* 1865. Intro. and Notes by Martin Gardner. New York: Bramhall, 1960.

Casey, Janet Galligani. "The Potential of Sisterhood: Christina Rossetti's *Goblin Market.*" *Victorian Poetry.* 29:1 (Spring, 1991): 63-78.

Chesterson, G.K. "Fairy Tales." *All Things Considered.* 2nd ed. London: Metheun, 1908.

Coleridge, Samuel Taylor. *Biographia Literaria.* 2 vols. Eds. James Engell and W. Jackson Bate. Princeton, NJ: Princeton University Press, 1983. Vol. 7 of *The Collected Works of Samuel Taylor Coleridge.* Kathleen Coburn, gen. ed. 14 vols. to date. 1971-1990.

———. *The Collected Letters of Samuel Taylor Coleridge.* Ed. E.L. Griggs. Oxford: Clarendon Press, 1956. 4 vols. 1956-1971.

———. "Dejection: An Ode." *The Complete Poetical Works of Samuel Taylor Coleridge.* Ed. Ernest Hartley Coleridge. 2 vols. Oxford: Clarendon, 1912. 1:362-8.

———. "The Eolian Harp." *The Complete Poetical Works.* 1: 100-102.

———. "Frost at Midnight." *The Complete Poetical Works.* 1: 240-42.

———. "Kubla Khan." *The Complete Poetical Works.* 1: 295-98.

———. "This Lime-Tree Bower My Prison." *The Complete Poetical Works.* 1: 178-81.

———. "The Rime of the Ancient Mariner." *The Complete Poetical Works.* 1: 186-209.

———. *Shakespearean Criticism.* Ed. Thomas Middleton Raysor. Vol. 2. 2 vols. Cambridge: Harvard University Press, 1930.

———. "The Statesman's Manual." *Lay Sermons.* Ed. R.J. White. Princeton, NJ: Princeton University Press, 1972. Vol. 6 of *The Collected Works of Samuel Taylor Coleridge.* Kathleen Coburn, gen. ed. 14 vols. to date. 1971-1990.

———. *Table Talk.* Ed. H.N. Coleridge. 1835. 4th ed. London: Murray, 1852.

Coleridge, Sara. *Memoir and Letters of Sara Coleridge.* Ed. Her Daughter (Edith Coleridge). 1874. New York: AMS, 1973.

Coyle, William. "Ruskin's *King of the Golden River*: A Victorian Fairy Tale." *The Scope of the Fantastic—Theory, Technique, Major Authors: Selected Essays from the First International Conference on the Fantastic in Literature and Film.* Eds. Robert A. Collins and Howard D. Pearce. Westport, CT: Greenwood, 1985. 85-90.

Darnton, Robert. "Peasants Tell Tales: The Meaning of Mother Goose." *The Great Cat Massacre and Other Episodes in French Cultural History.* New York: Basic Books, 1984. 9-10.

Darton, F. J. Harvey. *Children's Books in England: Five Centuries of Social Life.* 1932. 3rd ed. Rev. Brian Alderson. Cambridge: Cambridge University Press, 1982.

Dickens, Charles. "Frauds on the Fairies [Oct 1, 1853]." *Miscellaneous Papers, Plays and Poems.* Vol. 1. 2 vols. *The Works of Charles Dickens.* Vol. 18. 20 vols. New York: Bigelow, 1903. 392-400.

Egoff, Sheila A. *Worlds Within: Children's Fantasy from the Middle Ages to Today.* Chicago: American Library, 1988.

Ellis, John. *One Fairy Story Too Many: The Brothers Grimm and Their Tales.* Chicago: University of Chicago Press, 1983.

Ewing, Julianna Horatia. "Amelia and the Dwarves." Rpt. in *Forbidden Journeys: Fairy Tales and Fantasies by Victorian Women Writers.* Eds. Nina Auerbach and U.C. Knoepflmacher. Chicago: University of Chicago Press, 1992. 105-28.

Fleck, P.D. "Mary Shelley's Notes to Shelley's Poems and *Frankenstein.*" *Studies in Romanticism.* 6.4 (1967): 226-54.

Franz, Marie-Louise von. *The Problem of the Puer aeternus.* 1970. Rpt. As *Puer aeternus.* Santa Monica, CA: Sigo, 1981.

Freud, Sigmund. "The Uncanny." 1919. *Collected Papers.* Vol. 4. 1925. Trans. Joan Riviere. 5 vols. 1924-1950. London: Hogarth, 1950. 368-407.

Frye, Northrop. *The Secular Scripture: A Study of the Structure of Transcendence.* Cambridge: Harvard University Press, 1976.

Gardner, Martin. Notes. *The Annotated Alice: Alice's Adventures in Wonderland & Through the Looking Glass.* By Lewis Carroll. New York: Bramhall, 1960.

Gillin, Richard. "Romantic Echoes in the Willows." *Children's Literature.* 16 (1988): 169-74.

Gooderson, David. Introduction. *My Dearest Mouse: "The Wind in the Willows" Letters.* By Kenneth Grahame. London: Pavilion, 1988. 5-15.

Grahame, Kenneth. *Dream Days.* 1898. Berkeley: Ten Speed Press, 1993.

———. *Pagan Papers.* 1894. New York: Lane, 1902.

———. *The Wind in the Willows*. 1908. New York: Scribner, 1961.

Green, Peter. *Beyond the Wild Wood: The World of Kenneth Grahame*. New York: Facts on File, 1982.

Griffin, Andrew. "Fire and Ice in Frankenstein." *The Endurance of Frankenstein: Essays on Mary Shelley's Novel*. Eds. George Levine and U.C. Knoepflmacher. Berkeley, CA: University of California Press, 1974. 49-76.

Grimm, Jacob and Wilhelm. *The Complete Fairy Tales of the Brothers Grimm*. Trans. Jack Zipes. 1857 Ed. New York: Bantam, 1987.

Hein, Rolland. *The Harmony Within: The Spiritual Vision of George MacDonald*. Grand Rapids: Christian University Press, 1982.

Hertz, Neil. "The Notion of Blockage in the Literature of the Sublime." *Psychoanalysis and the Question of Text*. Ed. Geoffrey H. Hartman. Baltimore: Johns Hopkins, 1978.

Hunt, Peter. *The Wind in the Willows: A Fragmented Arcadia*. New York: Twayne, 1994.

Kingsley, Charles. *The Water Babies*. 1863. Bridlington, England: Haddock, n.d.

Kuznets, Lois R. "Kenneth Grahame and Father Nature, or Whither Blows *The Wind in The Willows?*" *Children's Literature*. 16 (1988): 175-84.

Lang, Andrew, Ed. *The Blue Fairy Book*. 1889. New York: Dover, 1965.

———. *The Red Fairy Book*. 1890. New York: Dover, 1966.

Le Guin, Ursula K. "From Elfland to Poughkeepsie." *The Language of the Night: Essays on Fantasy and Science Fiction*. Ed. Susan Wood. New York: Putnam, 1979.

Lewis, C.S. "On Three Ways of Writing for Children." 1952. *On Stories and Other Essays on Literature*. Ed. Walter Hooper. 1966. San Diego, CA: Harcourt, 1982.

Lurie, Alison. *Clever Gretchen and Other Forgotten Folktales*. London: Bloomsbury, 1990.

MacDonald, George. *At the Back of the North Wind*. 1871. New York: Puffin, 1986.

———. "The Fantastic Imagination." 1890. *A Dish of Orts: Chiefly Papers on the Imagination and on Shakespeare*. London: Dalton, 1908. 313-22.

———. *The Golden Key*. First Farrar Edition 1967. New York: Farrar, 1976.

———. "The Imagination: Its Function and Its Culture." *Orts*. 1-42.

———. *The Princess and Curdie*. 1882. New York: Puffin, 1966.

———. *The Princess and the Goblin*. 1872. New York: Puffin, 1964.

——. Epea aptera. *Unspoken Sermons*. Second Series. 1885. 3rd. ed. London: Strahan, 1869.

——. "Wordsworth's Poetry," *Orts*. 245-63.

MacLeod, Anne Scott. "From Rational to Romantic: The Children of Children's Literature in the Nineteenth-Century." *Poetics Today*. 13.1 (1992): 141-53.

Manlove, C.N. *The Impulse of Fantasy Literature*. Kent, OH: Kent State University Press, 1983.

——. "Victorian and Modern Fantasy." *The Celebration of the Fantastic: Selected Papers from the Tenth Anniversary International Conference on the Fantastic in the Arts*. Eds. Donald E. Morse, Marshall B. Tymn and Csilla Bertha. Westport, CT: Greenwood, 1992. 9-22.

Mellor, Anne K. *English Romantic Irony*. Cambridge, MA: Harvard University Press, 1980.

——. *Mary Shelley, Her Life, Her Fiction, Her Monsters*. New York: Methuen, 1988.

——. *Romanticism and Gender*. New York: Routledge, 1993.

Mendelson, Michael. "*The Wind in the Willows* and the Plotting of Contrast." *Children's Literature*. 16 (1988): 127-44.

Mermin, Dorothy. "Heroic Sisterhood in *Goblin Market.*" *Victorian Poetry*. 21:2 (1983): 107-18.

Modiano, Raimonda. *Coleridge and the Concept of Nature*. London: Macmillan, 1985.

Montgomery, Robert L. "Addison and the 'Helps and Ornaments of Art.'" *Criticism*. 25 (1983): 259-79.

Morris, David B. "Gothic Sublimity." *New Literary History*. 16.2 (1985): 299-320.

——. *The Religious Sublime*. Lexington, KY: University Press of Kentucky, 1972.

Opie, Iona and Peter. *The Classic Fairy Tales*. 1974. New York: Oxford University Press, 1992.

Perrault, Charles. "Cinderella: or, The Little Glass Slipper." *Histories or Tales of Past Times*. 1729. Rptd. in *The Classic Fairy Tales*. Ed. Iona and Peter Opie. 1974. New York: Oxford University Press, 1992. 123-7.

Pickering, Samuel F. *John Locke and Children's Books in Eighteenth Century England*. Knoxville, TN: University of Tennessee, 1981.

Poss, Geraldine D. "An Epic in Arcadia: The Pastoral World of *The Wind in the Willows.*" *Children's Literature*. 4 (1975): 80-90.

Prickett, Stephen. *Victorian Fantasy*. Bloomington, IN: Indiana

University Press, 1979.

Rabkin, Eric S. *The Fantastic in Literature*. Princeton, NJ: Princeton University Press, 1976.

Richardson, Alan. "Wordsworth, Fairy Tales, and the Politics of Children's Reading." *Romanticism and Children's Literature in Nineteenth-Century England*. Ed. James Holt McGavran, Jr. Athens, GA: University of Georgia, 1991. 34-53.

Rosenblum, Dolores. *Christina Rossetti: The Poetry of Endurance*. Carbondale, IL: Southern Illinois University Press, 1986.

Rossetti, Christina. *Goblin Market*. 1862. Toronto: Dover, 1983.

Rossetti, William Michael, Ed. Introduction. *The Poetical Works of Christina Georgina Rossetti*. London: Macmillan, 1904.

Sandor, Andras. "Myths and the Fantastic." *New Literary History*. 22.2 (1991): 339-58.

Siebers, Tobin. *The Romantic Fantastic*. Ithaca, NY: Cornell University Press, 1984.

Shawcross, John. "Coleridge Marginalia." *Notes and Queries*. 4 (1905): 341-2.

Shurbutt, Sylvia Bailey. "Revisionist Mythmaking in Christina Rossetti's 'Goblin Market': Eve's Apple and Other Questions Revised and Reconsidered." *Victorian Newsletter* 82 (1992): 40-4.

Tatar, Maria. *The Hard Facts of the Grimms' Fairy Tales*. Princeton, NJ: Princeton University Press, 1987.

———. *Off With Their Heads! Fairytales and the Culture of Childhood*. Princeton, NJ: Princeton University Press, 1992.

Taylor, Edgar, Trans. "Snow White." *German Popular Stories, Translated from the Kinder and Haus-Marchen, collected by M.M. Grimm, from Oral Tradition*. 1823. Rptd. in *The Classic Fairy Tales*. Ed. Iona and Peter Opie. 1974. New York: Oxford University Press, 1992. 177-82.

Tolkien, J.R.R. "On Fairy-Stories." 1938. *The Monsters and The Critics and Other Essays*. Ed. Christopher Tolkien. Boston: Houghton, 1984. 109-61.

Trimmer, Sarah. *The Guardian of Education*. 5 Vols. vol 1. London: Hatchard, 1802. 1802-6.

Watson, Jeanie. "'Men Sell Not Such in any Town': Christina Rossetti's Goblin Fruit of Fairy Tale." *Children's Literature: Annual of the Modern Language Association Division on Children's Literature and the Children's Literature Association*. Vol. 12. New Haven, CT: Yale University Press, 1984. 61-77.

———. "'The Raven: A Christmas Poem'—Coleridge and the Fairy Tale

Controversy." *Romanticism and Children's Literature in Nineteenth-Century England*. Ed. James Holt McGavran, Jr. Athens, GA: University of Georgia, 1991. 14-33.

Weiskel, Portia Williams. Foreword. *The Romantic Sublime: Studies in the Structure and Psychology of Transcendence*. Baltimore, MD: Johns Hopkins University Press, 1976.

Weiskel, Thomas. *The Romantic Sublime: Studies in the Structure and Psychology of Transcendence*. Baltimore, MD: Johns Hopkins University Press, 1976.

Wilde, Oscar. "The Selfish Giant." 1888. *Complete Works of Oscar Wilde*. 1948. London: Collins, 1966.

———. *The Letters of Oscar Wilde*. Ed. Rupert Hart-Davis. New York: Harcourt, 1962.

Wooden, Warren W. *Children's Literature of the English Renaissance*. Lexington, KY: University Press of Kentucky, 1986.

Woodman, Ross. "The Idiot Boy as Healer." *Romanticism and Children's Literature in Nineteenth-Century England*. Ed. James Holt McGavran, Jr. Athens, GA: University of Georgia, 1991. 72-95.

Wordsworth, William. "Anecdote for Fathers." *The Poetical Works of William Wordsworth*. Ed. Paul D. Sheets. Boston, MA: Houghton, 1982. 73-74.

———. Introduction. "Ode: Intimations of Immortality." *The Poetical Works*. 353.

———. "Ode: Intimations of Immortality." *The Poetical Works*. 353-6.

———. "Preface to the Lyrical Ballads." *The Poetical Works*. 790-99.

———. "My Heart Leaps Up." *The Poetical Works*. 277.

———. *The Prelude, 1799, 1805, 1850*. Eds. Jonathan Wordsworth, M.H. Abrams and Stephen Gill. New York: Norton, 1979.

———. "The Tables Turned." *The Poetical Works*. 83.

———. "Lines Composed a Few Miles above Tintern Abbey." *The Poetical Works*. 91-93.

———. "The World is Too Much With Us." *The Poetical Works*. 349.

Zipes, Jack. *Breaking the Magic Spell: Radical Theories of Folk and Fairy Tales*. Austin: University of Texas Press, 1979.

———. "Introduction." *The Complete Fairy Tales of the Brothers Grimm*. Trans. Jack Zipes. 1857 Ed. New York: Bantam, 1987.

Index

About the Author

DAVID SANDNER is a doctoral student at the University of Oregon, studying Romantic poetry and nineteenth-century fantastic literature. He received his B.A. from the University of California at Santa Cruz, and his M.A. from San Francisco State University.

ISBN 0-313-30084-4

HARDCOVER BAR CODE